TEN
THINGS
YOU
NEED
TO KNOW

About the Children's Market

TEN THINGS YOU NEED TO KNOW

About the Children's Market

BY THE NEW STRATEGIST EDITORS

New Strategist Publications, Inc.
Ithaca, New York

New Strategist Publications, Inc.
P.O. Box 242, Ithaca, New York 14851
800/848-0842; 607/273-0913
www.newstrategist.com

ISBN 978-1-933588-96-4
ISBN 1-933588-96-9

Printed in the United States of America

Table of Contents

List of Tables

Fact #8 The Children's Market Is Multiracial

Fact #9 The Children's Market Is Local

Fact #10 Parental Aspirations Are Key

Appendices

List of Charts

Fact #8 The Children's Market Is Multiracial

Fact #9 The Children's Market Is Local

Fact #10 Parental Aspirations Are Key

Introduction

Marketing to children today is a challenge. Not only are children harder to find in our aging nation, but children themselves are becoming more diverse in every way. *Ten Things You Need to Know about the Children's Market* is designed to help you focus your efforts on the most important demographic trends occurring among children and their families.

Ten Things You Need to Know about the Children's Market is meant to fill a gaping hole in business research. Too often, businesses do not understand the basics about their markets. Overwhelmed by the trees—brand names, sales figures, psychographics, etc.—they can miss the forest. When marketers allow details to overwhelm them, they risk ignoring what is most important about their market. This report is meant to provide marketers with the demographic context, a context into which all other market research can be placed.

For those creating programs, policies, or products for children, *Ten Things You Need to Know about the Children's Market* has the facts you need to jump-start your research. Each of the points discussed on the following pages is accompanied by explanatory charts and easy-to-read tables, bringing you up to date on the trends. Those who want to delve deeper can access the sources listed at the bottom of each table and in the bibliography. The listed links will take you to the government's voluminous demographic databases.

Ten Things You Need to Know about the Children's Market is a starting point, a refresher course, a reality check, and an idea generator. It is another tool for capturing customers.

Fact #1

The Children's Market Is a Moving Target

The children's market is rapidly changing, making it a moving target. In the United States, the percentage of households that include children is shrinking, which means it is more important than ever to aim carefully. Less than one-third of households today include children under age 18, down from nearly half in 1950. Each year, the percentage of households with children shrinks a little more.

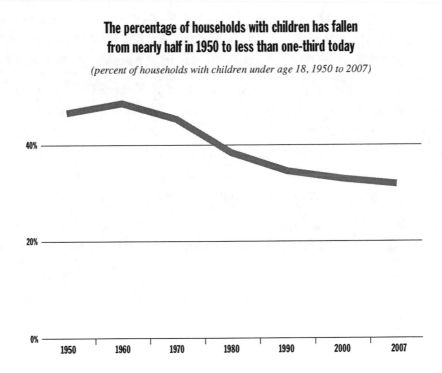

The percentage of households with children has fallen from nearly half in 1950 to less than one-third today

(percent of households with children under age 18, 1950 to 2007)

Children are found in fewer households for several reasons. One, the population is aging. Consequently, more householders are well beyond the family formation years. Two, because the typical family has only one or two children today—down from three or four children in the 1950s—the childrearing years are shorter and the empty-nest years longer. Critics sometimes fault children (and their parents) for children's increasingly sedentary lifestyle. But there may be a good reason the kids no longer play outside. Because so few households include children, playmates are scarce in many neighborhoods.

The percentage of households with children varies greatly by race and Hispanic origin. Among Hispanic households, nearly half include children under age 18. Among non-Hispanic white households, the figure is just 28 percent. This means Hispanic households are nearly twice as likely as non-Hispanic white households to include children.

Hispanic households are much more likely to include children than Asian, black, or non-Hispanic white households

(percent of households with children under age 18, by race and Hispanic origin of householder, 2007)

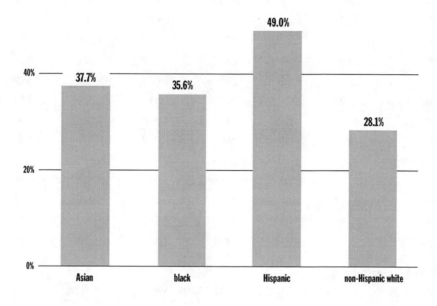

CONSIDER THESE POINTS

■ Because most households do not include children, mass marketing is inefficient for reaching children and their parents.

■ The search by parents for child-friendly neighborhoods is one factor behind the mushrooming suburban sprawl surrounding most American cities.

■ The growing number of Hispanics in the United States may slow the decline in households with children.

Table 1.1. Households with Children under Age 18 by Household Type, 1950 to 2007

(number and percent distribution of households by presence of own children under age 18 at home, 1950 to 2007; numbers in thousands)

| | total households | families with children under age 18 | | | | |
| | | total | married couples | single parent | | |
				total	mother only	father only
Number						
2007	116,011	36,757	26,158	10,600	8,585	2,015
2006	114,384	36,466	25,982	10,484	8,389	2,095
2005	113,343	36,211	25,919	10,291	8,270	2,021
2004	112,000	35,944	25,793	10,152	8,221	1,931
2003	111,278	35,968	25,914	10,054	8,139	1,915
2002	109,297	35,705	25,792	9,913	8,010	1,903
2001	108,209	35,355	25,980	9,374	7,538	1,836
2000	104,705	34,605	25,248	9,357	7,571	1,786
1990	93,347	32,289	24,537	7,752	6,599	1,153
1980	80,776	31,022	24,961	6,061	5,445	616
1970	63,401	28,812	25,541	3,271	2,971	345
1960	52,799	25,690	23,358	2,332	2,099	232
1950	43,554	20,324	18,824	1,500	1,272	229
Percent distribution						
2007	100.0%	31.7%	22.5%	9.1%	7.4%	1.7%
2006	100.0	31.9	22.7	9.2	7.3	1.8
2005	100.0	31.9	22.9	9.1	7.3	1.8
2004	100.0	32.1	23.0	9.1	7.3	1.7
2003	100.0	32.3	23.3	9.0	7.3	1.7
2002	100.0	32.7	23.6	9.1	7.3	1.7
2001	100.0	32.7	24.0	8.7	7.0	1.7
2000	100.0	33.0	24.1	8.9	7.2	1.7
1990	100.0	34.6	26.3	8.3	7.1	1.2
1980	100.0	38.4	30.9	7.5	6.7	0.8
1970	100.0	45.4	40.3	5.2	4.7	0.5
1960	100.0	48.7	44.2	4.4	4.0	0.4
1950	100.0	46.7	43.2	3.4	2.9	0.5

Source: Bureau of the Census, Families and Living Arrangements, Historical Tables—Households, Internet site http://www .census.gov/population/www/socdemo/hh-fam.html; calculations by New Strategist

Table 1.2 Households with Children by Race and Hispanic Origin, 2007

(number and percent distribution of total households by presence of own children under age 18, by race and Hispanic origin of householder, 2007; numbers in thousands)

	number	families with children	
		number	percent
Total households	**116,011**	**36,757**	**31.7%**
Asian	4,664	1,756	37.7
Black	14,709	5,235	35.6
Hispanic	12,973	6,356	49.0
Non-Hispanic white	82,675	23,213	28.1

Source: Bureau of the Census, America's Families and Living Arrangements, 2007, Internet site http://www.census.gov/population/www/socdemo/hh-fam/cps2007.html; calculations by New Strategist

Fact #2

The Children's Market Is Fragmented

Few households in the United States are experiencing the stereotypical bustle of family life. Among the nation's 114 million households, 68 percent have no children under age 18 in the home, 13 percent have one child, and 18 percent have two or more.

Most households have no children

(percent distribution of total households by presence and number of children, 2007)

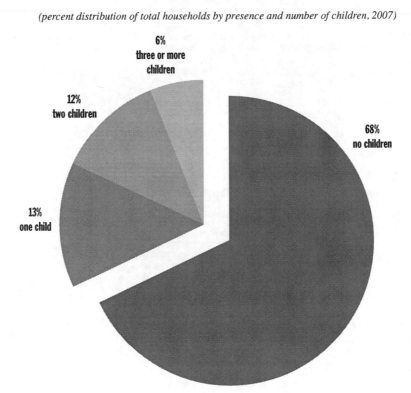

Many households with only one child at home are approaching the empty-nest years and have an older child in college or living independently.

Hispanic households are the most child oriented. Thirty-one percent of Hispanic households include two or more children compared with only 16 percent of all non-Hispanic white households.

Nearly one-third of all Hispanic households include two or more children

(households with two or more children as a percentage of total households, by race and Hispanic origin, 2007)

[Bar chart showing percentages by race and Hispanic origin: Asian 21%, black 20%, Hispanic 31%, non-Hispanic white 16%. Y-axis ranges from 0% to 30%.]

Because Hispanics are, on average, younger than non-Hispanic whites and their families are larger, they are more likely to be knee-deep in the childrearing stage of life. Non-Hispanic white households with children are more likely to be approaching the empty-nest years.

Demographically speaking, the children's market is no monolith, but fragmented into many separate segments because of the different wants and needs of children (and their parents) by age. The 37 million households with children split almost evenly into three segments by the age of children in the home. Seventeen million households include teenagers, another 17 million include children aged 6 to 11, and 16 million include preschoolers.

Among families with children, nearly half include a preschooler,
nearly half include a preteen, and nearly half include a teenager

(percent of families with children under age 18 by age of children in any age group, 2007; numbers add up to more than 100 percent because many families include children in more than one age group)

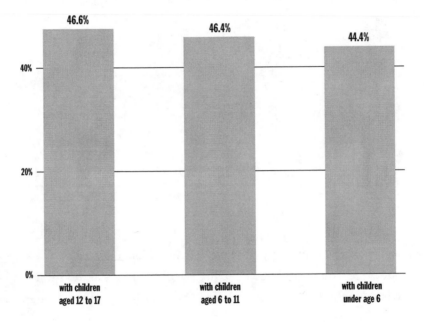

Looked at another way, however, the segments change in size. The 56 percent majority of families with children have *only* school-aged children in the home. Another 24 percent have *only* preschoolers at home, and the smallest share has *both* preschoolers and school-aged children.

Among families with children, only 20 percent include both preschoolers and schooled-aged children

(percent of families with children under age 18 by age of children in exclusive age groups, 2007)

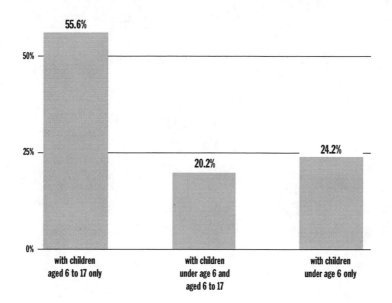

CONSIDER THESE POINTS

■ If you are looking for the stereotypical family, target the Hispanic population. Even among Hispanics, however, most households have no children or only one child.

■ Although the average American lives a child-free lifestyle, keep in mind that many have grown children—and grandchildren—living elsewhere. Among people aged 50 to 64, the 56 percent majority has grandchildren, and the figure rises as high as 82 percent among people aged 65 or older, according to a Pew Research Center survey.

■ Most families with children are involved with the local schools, since the majority has school-aged children. Far from being dissatisfied with their local schools, most parents give the school their child attends a grade of A or B, according to the annual Phi Delta Kappa/Gallup Poll of the Public's Attitudes toward the Public Schools.

Table 2.1 Households by Age of Householder and Number of Children, 2007

(number and percent distribution of households by age of householder and number of own children under age 18 living at home, 2007; numbers in thousands)

	total	with one or more children under age 18				
		total	one	two	three	four or more
Total households	**116,011**	**36,757**	**15,651**	**13,815**	**5,188**	**2,104**
Under age 20	916	150	127	21	2	0
Aged 20 to 24	5,746	1,752	1,087	520	112	32
Aged 25 to 29	9,667	4,370	1,894	1,589	628	260
Aged 30 to 34	9,767	5,975	1,976	2,467	1,040	491
Aged 35 to 39	10,841	7,439	2,265	3,152	1,418	603
Aged 40 to 44	11,938	7,317	2,688	3,047	1,144	438
Aged 45 to 49	12,604	5,503	2,784	1,932	597	190
Aged 50 to 54	11,537	2,774	1,788	746	181	58
Aged 55 to 64	19,266	1,274	894	294	59	26
Aged 65 to 74	11,926	156	115	32	7	3
Aged 75 or older	11,803	47	32	14	0	1
Percent distribution by number of children						
Total households	**100.0%**	**31.7%**	**13.5%**	**11.9%**	**4.5%**	**1.8%**
Under age 20	100.0	16.4	13.9	2.3	0.2	0.0
Aged 20 to 24	100.0	30.5	18.9	9.0	1.9	0.6
Aged 25 to 29	100.0	45.2	19.6	16.4	6.5	2.7
Aged 30 to 34	100.0	61.2	20.2	25.3	10.6	5.0
Aged 35 to 39	100.0	68.6	20.9	29.1	13.1	5.6
Aged 40 to 44	100.0	61.3	22.5	25.5	9.6	3.7
Aged 45 to 49	100.0	43.7	22.1	15.3	4.7	1.5
Aged 50 to 54	100.0	24.0	15.5	6.5	1.6	0.5
Aged 55 to 64	100.0	6.6	4.6	1.5	0.3	0.1
Aged 65 to 74	100.0	1.3	1.0	0.3	0.1	0.0
Aged 75 or older	100.0	0.4	0.3	0.1	0.0	0.0

Source: Bureau of the Census, America's Families and Living Arrangements, 2007, Internet site http://www.census.gov/ population/www/socdemo/hh-fam/cps2007.html; calculations by New Strategist

Table 2.2 Households by Race, Hispanic Origin, and Number of Children, 2007

(number and percent distribution of total households and households with own children under age 18, by race and Hispanic origin of householder, 2007; numbers in thousands)

	number	Asians	blacks	Hispanics	non-Hispanic whites
Total households	**116,011**	**4,664**	**14,709**	**12,973**	**82,675**
With children under age 18	36,757	1,756	5,235	6,356	23,213
One child	15,651	764	2,363	2,354	10,091
Two children	13,815	747	1,727	2,401	8,871
Three children	5,188	184	741	1,094	3,144
Four or more children	2,104	61	405	507	1,108
Percent distribution					
Total households	**100.0%**	**100.0%**	**100.0%**	**100.0%**	**100.0%**
With children under age 18	31.7	37.7	35.6	49.0	28.1
One child	13.5	16.4	16.1	18.1	12.2
Two children	11.9	16.0	11.7	18.5	10.7
Three children	4.5	3.9	5.0	8.4	3.8
Four or more children	1.8	1.3	2.8	3.9	1.3

Note: Asians and blacks are those who identify themselves as being of the race alone or as being of the race in combination with other races. Non-Hispanic whites are those who identify themselves as being white alone and not Hispanic. Hispanics may be of any race. Numbers will not add to total because not all races are shown.
Source: Bureau of the Census, America's Families and Living Arrangements, 2007, Internet site http://www.census.gov/population/www/socdemo/hh-fam/cps2007.html; calculations by New Strategist

Table 2.3 Households with Children in Any Age Group by Age of Householder, 2007

(number and percent distribution of households with own children under age 18 by age of householder and age of own children in any age group, and mean age of householder, 2007; numbers in thousands)

	total	12 to 17	6 to 11	under 6
Total households with children	**36,757**	**17,142**	**17,046**	**16,306**
Under age 20	150	0	10	143
Aged 20 to 24	1,752	4	221	1,681
Aged 25 to 29	4,370	269	1,965	3,647
Aged 30 to 34	5,975	1,489	3,245	4,137
Aged 35 to 39	7,439	3,325	4,329	3,637
Aged 40 to 44	7,317	4,550	4,009	1,942
Aged 45 to 49	5,503	4,148	2,176	695
Aged 50 to 54	2,774	2,216	728	243
Aged 55 to 64	1,274	1,000	305	147
Aged 65 to 74	156	116	37	27
Aged 75 or older	47	25	20	9
Mean age (years)	39.2	43.7	38.5	33.6
Percent distribution				
Total households with children	**100.0%**	**46.6%**	**46.4%**	**44.4%**
Under age 20	100.0	0.0	6.7	95.3
Aged 20 to 24	100.0	0.2	12.6	95.9
Aged 25 to 29	100.0	6.2	45.0	83.5
Aged 30 to 34	100.0	24.9	54.3	69.2
Aged 35 to 39	100.0	44.7	58.2	48.9
Aged 40 to 44	100.0	62.2	54.8	26.5
Aged 45 to 49	100.0	75.4	39.5	12.6
Aged 50 to 54	100.0	79.9	26.2	8.8
Aged 55 to 64	100.0	78.5	23.9	11.5
Aged 65 to 74	100.0	74.4	23.7	17.3
Aged 75 or older	100.0	53.2	42.6	19.1

Note: Numbers will not add to total because many households have children in more than one age group.
Source: Bureau of the Census, America's Families and Living Arrangements, 2007, Internet site http://www.census.gov/population/www/socdemo/hh-fam/cps2007.html; calculations by New Strategist

Table 2.4 Households with Children in Any Age Group by Race and Hispanic Origin of Householder, 2007

(number and percent distribution of households with own children under age 18 by age of children in any age group, and race and Hispanic origin of householder, 2007; numbers in thousands)

	total	Asians	blacks	Hispanics	non-Hispanic whites
Total households with children	**36,757**	**1,756**	**5,235**	**6,356**	**23,213**
Under age 6	17,142	845	2,284	3,259	9,867
Aged 6 to 11	17,046	783	2,509	3,263	10,405
Aged 12 to 17	16,306	713	2,563	2,855	10,881
Percent distribution					
Total households with children	**100.0%**	**100.0%**	**100.0%**	**100.0%**	**100.0%**
Under age 6	46.6	48.1	43.6	51.3	42.5
Aged 6 to 11	46.4	44.6	47.9	51.3	44.8
Aged 12 to 17	44.4	40.6	49.0	44.9	46.9

Note: Numbers will not add to total because many households have children in more than one age group and because not all races are shown. Asians and blacks are those who identify themselves as being of the race alone or as being of the race in combination with other races. Non-Hispanic whites are those who identify themselves as being white alone and not Hispanic. Hispanics may be of any race.
Source: Bureau of the Census, America's Families and Living Arrangements, 2007, Internet site http://www.census.gov/ population/www/socdemo/hh-fam/cps2007.html; calculations by New Strategist

Table 2.5 Households with Children in Exclusive Age Groups by Age of Householder, 2007

(number and percent distribution of households with own children under age 18 by age of householder and age of children in exclusive age groups, and mean age of householder, 2007; numbers in thousands)

	total	under 6 only	some under 6, some 6 to 17	6 to 17 only
Total households with children	**36,757**	**8,882**	**7,424**	**20,451**
Under age 20	150	141	2	8
Aged 20 to 24	1,752	1,528	154	71
Aged 25 to 29	4,370	2,307	1,340	723
Aged 30 to 34	5,975	2,183	1,954	1,837
Aged 35 to 39	7,439	1,525	2,112	3,802
Aged 40 to 44	7,317	684	1,257	5,376
Aged 45 to 49	5,503	264	430	4,808
Aged 50 to 54	2,774	135	108	2,531
Aged 55 to 64	1,274	93	54	1,127
Aged 65 to 74	156	16	11	130
Aged 75 or older	47	7	2	39
Mean age (years)	39.2	31.8	35.6	43.3
Percent distribution				
Total households with children	**100.0%**	**24.2%**	**20.2%**	**55.6%**
Under age 20	100.0	94.0	1.3	5.3
Aged 20 to 24	100.0	87.2	8.8	4.1
Aged 25 to 29	100.0	52.8	30.7	16.5
Aged 30 to 34	100.0	36.5	32.7	30.7
Aged 35 to 39	100.0	20.5	28.4	51.1
Aged 40 to 44	100.0	9.3	17.2	73.5
Aged 45 to 49	100.0	4.8	7.8	87.4
Aged 50 to 54	100.0	4.9	3.9	91.2
Aged 55 to 64	100.0	7.3	4.2	88.5
Aged 65 to 74	100.0	10.3	7.1	83.3
Aged 75 or older	100.0	14.9	4.3	83.0

Source: Bureau of the Census, America's Families and Living Arrangements, 2007, Internet site http://www.census.gov/ population/www/socdemo/hh-fam/cps2007.html; calculations by New Strategist

Table 2.6 Households with Children in Exclusive Age Groups by Race and Hispanic Origin of Householder, 2007

(number and percent distribution of households with own children under age 18 by age of children in exclusive age groups and race and Hispanic origin of householder, 2007; numbers in thousands)

	total	Asians	blacks	Hispanics	non-Hispanic whites
Total households with children	**36,757**	**1,756**	**5,235**	**6,356**	**23,213**
Under age 6 only	8,882	511	1,110	1,524	5,720
Some under 6, some 6 to 17	7,424	333	1,175	1,735	4,147
Aged 6 to 17 only	20,451	911	2,951	3,098	13,346
Percent distribution					
Total households with children	**100.0%**	**100.0%**	**100.0%**	**100.0%**	**100.0%**
Under age 6 only	24.2	29.1	21.2	24.0	24.6
Some under 6, some 6 to 17	20.2	19.0	22.4	27.3	17.9
Aged 6 to 17 only	55.6	51.9	56.4	48.7	57.5

Note: Asians and blacks are those who identify themselves as being of the race alone or as being of the race in combination with other races. Non-Hispanic whites are those who identify themselves as being white alone and not Hispanic. Hispanics may be of any race. Numbers will not add to total because not all races are shown.
Source: Bureau of the Census, America's Families and Living Arrangements, 2007, Internet site http://www.census.gov/ population/www/socdemo/hh-fam/cps2007.html; calculations by New Strategist

Fact #3

Generation X Dominates Households with Children

There is a shortcut to targeting the children's market today: focus on Generation X. Not only does Generation X head the largest share of households with children, but most Generation X householders have children at home.

The nation's parents are likely to be Generation Xers

(percent distribution of households with children under age 18, by generation of householder, 2007)

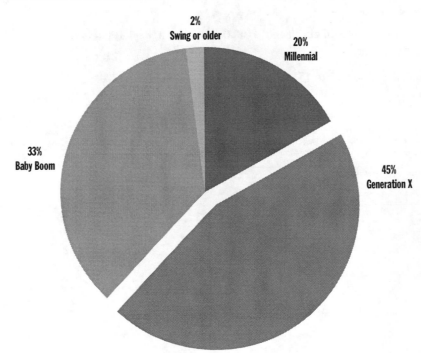

Nearly half (45 percent) of the nation's 37 million households with children under age 18 are headed by members of Generation X—which spanned the ages from 31 to 42 in 2007. Only 20 percent of households with children are headed by the younger Millennial generation (under age 31). Boomers (aged 43 to 61) still head a substantial share of households with children, but their 33 percent share is rapidly shrinking.

On most family issues, the attitudes of Gen Xers match those of Boomers. Both support working women, according to the General Social Survey.

Gen Xers and Boomers support working women

(percent who disagree that it is better for a man to work and a woman to tend the home, 2006)

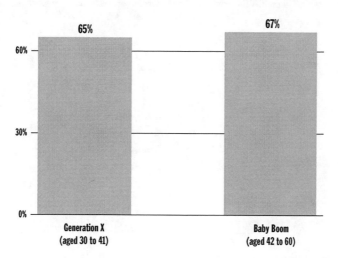

They also firmly support working mothers

(percent who agree that a working mother does not hurt her children, 2006)

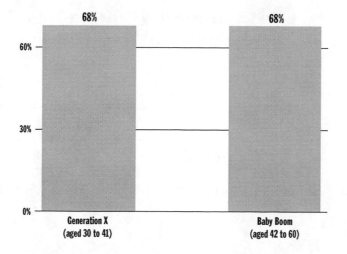

The attitudes of Generation Xers and Boomers toward childrearing are also similar. Both generations believe it is more important for children to learn to think for themselves rather than to obey.

Gen Xers and Boomers believe children should think for themselves

(percent who say thinking for oneself is the first- or second-most important trait children should be taught, 2006)

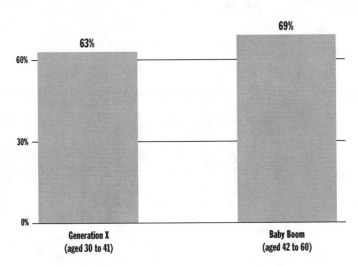

But Gen Xers are slightly more traditional in their childrearing practices. They are more likely than Boomers to think obedience is an important trait to instill in children.

But Gen Xers believe more strongly in obedience

(percent who say obedience is the first- or second-most important trait children should be taught, 2006)

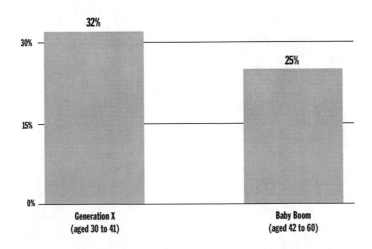

Generation Xers place more importance on obedience because they are more likely than Boomers to be black or Hispanic, and blacks and Hispanics are more likely than non-Hispanic whites to regard obedience as an important trait.

Another factor that differentiates Generation X from Boomer parents is their personal outlook. Generation Xers are significantly more optimistic than Boomers about their children's future.

Gen Xers are more optimistic

(percent who agree that their children's standard of living will be better than their own, 2006)

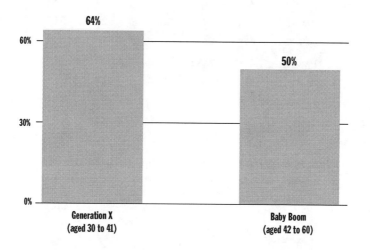

One reason why Generation Xers are more optimistic than Boomers is that a larger share are immigrants, and many immigrants have experienced socioeconomic gains since arriving in the United States. They foresee more gains ahead for their children.

CONSIDER THESE POINTS

■ Marketing campaigns that appeal to Generation X are likely to reach today's parents, since 64 percent of Generation X households include children.

■ While Boomer parents may be wringing their hands about their children's future, Generation Xers are much more optimistic. Feeding their hope is an important way to appeal to Generation X.

Table 3.1 Households by Age of Householder, Type of Household, and Presence of Children, 2007

(number and percent distribution of households by age of householder, type of household, and presence of own children under age 18, and mean age of householder, 2007; numbers in thousands)

	all households		married couples		female-headed families		male-headed families	
	total	with children	total	with children	total	with children	total	with children
Total households	**116,011**	**36,757**	**58,945**	**25,982**	**14,416**	**8,389**	**5,063**	**2,095**
Under age 20	916	150	59	36	285	98	261	9
Aged 20 to 24	5,746	1,752	1,295	824	1,044	883	591	152
Aged 25 to 29	9,667	4,370	3,920	2,649	1,629	1,312	665	282
Aged 30 to 34	9,767	5,975	5,461	4,389	1,514	1,425	479	315
Aged 35 to 39	10,841	7,439	6,492	5,379	1,742	1,575	465	355
Aged 40 to 44	11,938	7,317	6,879	5,486	1,909	1,484	565	383
Aged 45 to 49	12,604	5,503	7,169	4,119	1,662	943	601	297
Aged 50 to 54	11,537	2,774	6,644	2,013	1,267	435	465	194
Aged 55 to 64	19,266	1,274	10,910	947	1,530	192	535	87
Aged 65 to 74	11,926	156	6,155	108	912	31	216	18
Aged 75 or older	11,803	47	3,960	33	922	12	220	3
Mean age (years)	49.3	38.6	49.3	39.4	44.1	36.2	41.0	38.7

Percent distribution by age of householder

	all households		married couples		female-headed families		male-headed families	
Total households	**100.0%**	**100.0%**	**100.0%**	**100.0%**	**100.0%**	**100.0%**	**100.0%**	**100.0%**
Under age 20	0.8	0.4	0.1	0.1	2.0	1.2	5.2	0.4
Aged 20 to 24	5.0	4.8	2.2	3.2	7.2	10.5	11.7	7.3
Aged 25 to 29	8.3	11.9	6.7	10.2	11.3	15.6	13.1	13.5
Aged 30 to 34	8.4	16.3	9.3	16.9	10.5	17.0	9.5	15.0
Aged 35 to 39	9.3	20.2	11.0	20.7	12.1	18.8	9.2	16.9
Aged 40 to 44	10.3	19.9	11.7	21.1	13.2	17.7	11.2	18.3
Aged 45 to 49	10.9	15.0	12.2	15.9	11.5	11.2	11.9	14.2
Aged 50 to 54	9.9	7.5	11.3	7.7	8.8	5.2	9.2	9.3
Aged 55 to 64	16.6	3.5	18.5	3.6	10.6	2.3	10.6	4.2
Aged 65 to 74	10.3	0.4	10.4	0.4	6.3	0.4	4.3	0.9
Aged 75 or older	10.2	0.1	6.7	0.1	6.4	0.1	4.3	0.1

(continued)

	all households		married couples		female-headed families		male-headed families	
	total	with children	total	with children	total	with children	total	with children
Percent of households with children by type								
Total households	**100.0%**	**31.7%**	**100.0%**	**44.1%**	**100.0%**	**58.2%**	**100.0%**	**41.4%**
Under age 20	100.0	16.4	100.0	61.0	100.0	34.4	100.0	3.4
Aged 20 to 24	100.0	30.5	100.0	63.6	100.0	84.6	100.0	25.7
Aged 25 to 29	100.0	45.2	100.0	67.6	100.0	80.5	100.0	42.4
Aged 30 to 34	100.0	61.2	100.0	80.4	100.0	94.1	100.0	65.8
Aged 35 to 39	100.0	68.6	100.0	82.9	100.0	90.4	100.0	76.3
Aged 40 to 44	100.0	61.3	100.0	79.7	100.0	77.7	100.0	67.8
Aged 45 to 49	100.0	43.7	100.0	57.5	100.0	56.7	100.0	49.4
Aged 50 to 54	100.0	24.0	100.0	30.3	100.0	34.3	100.0	41.7
Aged 55 to 64	100.0	6.6	100.0	8.7	100.0	12.5	100.0	16.3
Aged 65 to 74	100.0	1.3	100.0	1.8	100.0	3.4	100.0	8.3
Aged 75 or older	100.0	0.4	100.0	0.8	100.0	1.3	100.0	1.4

Source: Bureau of the Census, America's Families and Living Arrangements, 2007, Internet site http://www.census.gov/ population/www/socdemo/hh-fam/cps2007.html; calculations by New Strategist

Table 3.2 Households by Generation of Householder, Type of Household, and Presence of Children, 2007

(number and percent distribution of households by generation of householder, type of household, and presence of own children under age 18, 2007; numbers in thousands)

	all households		married couples		female-headed families		male-headed families	
	total	with children	total	with children	total	with children	total	with children
Total households	**116,011**	**36,757**	**58,945**	**25,982**	**14,416**	**8,389**	**5,063**	**2,095**
Millennial (15 to 30)	18,282	7,467	6,366	4,387	3,261	2,578	1,613	506
Generation X (31 to 42)	25,817	16,609	14,988	12,182	4,099	3,605	1,187	837
Baby Boom (43 to 61)	42,402	12,096	24,202	8,989	4,764	2,106	1,667	705
Swing (62 to 74)	17,706	538	9,428	392	1,371	89	377	44
World War II (75 or older)	11,803	47	3,960	33	922	12	220	3
Percent distribution by generation of householder								
Total households	**100.0%**	**100.0%**	**100.0%**	**100.0%**	**100.0%**	**100.0%**	**100.0%**	**100.0%**
Millennial (15 to 30)	15.8	20.3	10.8	16.9	22.6	30.7	31.9	24.2
Generation X (31 to 42)	22.3	45.2	25.4	46.9	28.4	43.0	23.4	39.9
Baby Boom (43 to 61)	36.6	32.9	41.1	34.6	33.0	25.1	32.9	33.7
Swing (62 to 74)	15.3	1.5	16.0	1.5	9.5	1.1	7.4	2.1
World War II (75 or older)	10.2	0.1	6.7	0.1	6.4	0.1	4.3	0.1
Percent of households with children by type								
Total households	**100.0%**	**31.7%**	**100.0%**	**44.1%**	**100.0%**	**58.2%**	**100.0%**	**41.4%**
Millennial (15 to 30)	100.0	40.8	100.0	68.9	100.0	79.1	100.0	31.4
Generation X (31 to 42)	100.0	64.3	100.0	81.3	100.0	88.0	100.0	70.5
Baby Boom (43 to 61)	100.0	28.5	100.0	37.1	100.0	44.2	100.0	42.3
Swing (62 to 74)	100.0	3.0	100.0	4.2	100.0	6.5	100.0	11.7
World War II (75 or older)	100.0	0.4	100.0	0.8	100.0	1.3	100.0	1.4

Note: Number of households by generation are estimates by New Strategist.
Source: Bureau of the Census, America's Families and Living Arrangements: 2007, Internet site http://www.census.gov/population/www/socdemo/hh-fam/cps2007.html; calculations by New Strategist

Fact #4

Family Life Runs on a Schedule

For the majority of families with children, life can best be described as hectic. Among married couples with children, both parents are employed in the 62 percent majority. Among female-headed families, mom is employed in an even larger 73 percent. Among male-headed families, 85 percent of dads are in the labor force.

Most parents work

(percent of families with children under age 18 in which all parents in the household are employed, by family type, 2007)

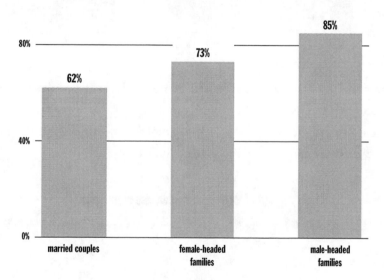

Most children today do not have a stay-at-home mom to look after them. Consequently, children's lives are as heavily scheduled as their parents' lives, with day care, before- and after-school activities, sports, clubs, and playdates planned well in advance. Today's families have little opportunity for spontaneous fun.

No matter how young the child, most women are at work. Even among infants, more than half of mothers are in the labor force.

Three out of four mothers of school-aged children are employed

(labor force participation rate of women with children under age 18, by age of youngest child, 2007)

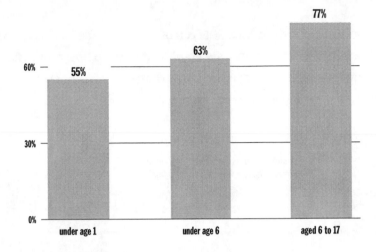

With mothers and fathers at work, most households with children have no parent solely dedicated to managing family life. The result is more chaos, less free time, and a greater blurring of sex roles than in the decades before most mothers went to work. Working parents have made day care, two cars, and a dependence on fast food the norm.

Nearly two out of three preschoolers are in day care

(percent of children aged 0 to 6 who are not yet in kindergarten by type of care arrangement, 2005)

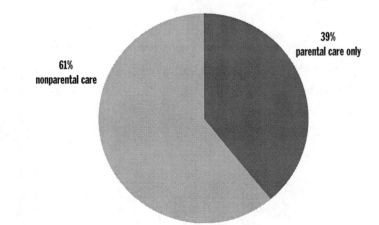

Child care needs are important for parents with school-aged children. Among children in kindergarten through eighth grade, about half are in nonparental care before or after school at least some of the time.

Although most parents work, children are not being short-changed. Time use studies show that today's mothers spend even more time with their children than mothers did a generation ago, despite the fact that more mothers are in the labor force.

Mothers and fathers are spending more time with their children

(hours per week spent providing child care as a primary activity by married parents, 1965 and 2000)

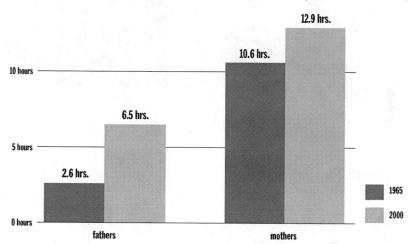

Source: Bianchi, Suzanne M., John P. Robinson, and Melissa A. Milkie. Table 4.1, "Weekly Hours of Child Care." In Changing Rhythms of American Family Life. © 2006 Russell Sage Foundation, 112 East 64th Street, New York, NY 10021. Reprinted with permission.

Mothers have managed to increase the time they spend with their children by reducing their housework, and fathers are doing more around the house to make up the difference. The lifestyle of today's parents is much more egalitarian than in the past.

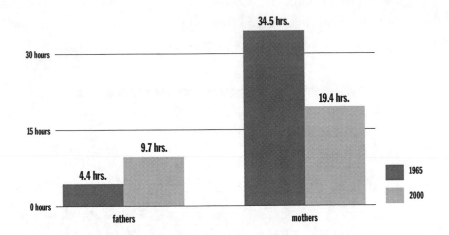

Mothers are spending less time doing housework, fathers more

(hours per week spent doing housework as a primary activity by married parents, 1965 and 2000)

Source: Suzanne M. Bianchi et al., *Changing Rhythms of American Family Life* (New York: Russell Sage Foundation, 2006)

CONSIDER THESE POINTS

■ With the cost of a middle-class lifestyle rising faster than incomes, few families can afford the luxury of a stay-at-home mom.

■ Although the lifestyle of today's parents is more egalitarian, women are still more likely than men to manage the family schedule. This makes mothers rather than fathers the primary family decision makers.

■ One of the best ways to reach children and their parents is through day care and after-school programs.

Table 4.1 Employment Status of Parents, 2007

(number and percent distribution of families with own children under age 18 at home, by age of children, family type, and employment status of parent, 2007; numbers in thousands; families in which all parents are employed denoted in bold)

	number	percent
Families with children, total		
Married couples	25,125	100.0%
Both parents employed	**15,627**	**62.2**
Father only employed	7,604	30.3
Mother only employed	1,228	4.9
Neither parent employed	666	2.7
Female-headed families	8,554	100.0
Mother employed	**6,224**	**72.8**
Mother not employed	2,330	27.2
Male-headed families	2,177	100.0
Father employed	**1,855**	**85.2**
Father not employed	322	14.8
Families with children aged 6 to 17		
Married couples	13,823	100.0
Both parents employed	**9,341**	**67.6**
Father only employed	3,309	23.9
Mother only employed	785	5.7
Neither parent employed	388	2.8
Female-headed families	5,224	100.0
Mother employed	**4,070**	**77.9**
Mother not employed	1,155	22.1
Male-headed families	1,314	100.0
Father employed	**1,115**	**84.9**
Father not employed	199	15.1
Families with children under age 6		
Married couples	11,302	100.0
Both parents employed	**6,287**	**55.6**
Father only employed	4,295	38.0
Mother only employed	442	3.9
Neither parent employed	278	2.5
Female-headed families	3,329	100.0
Mother employed	**2,154**	**64.7**
Mother not employed	1,175	35.3
Male-headed families	863	100.0
Father employed	**740**	**85.7**
Father not employed	123	14.3

Source: Bureau of Labor Statistics, Employment Characteristics of Families, Internet site http://www.bls.gov/news.release/ famee.toc.htm

Talbe 4.2 Labor Force Status of Women by Presence of Children, 2007

(number and percent distribution of women by labor force status and presence and age of own children under age 18 at home, 2007; numbers in thousands)

	civilian population	civilian labor force total	employed total	full-time	part-time
Total women	**119,694**	**70,988**	**67,792**	**51,056**	**16,736**
No children under age 18	82,577	44,620	42,635	32,003	10,632
With children under age 18	37,117	26,368	25,157	19,053	6,104
Children aged 6 to 17, none younger	20,599	15,910	15,310	11,910	3,400
Children under age 6	16,518	10,458	9,847	7,143	2,704
Children under age 3	9,659	5,721	5,354	3,783	1,571
Children under age 1	3,346	1,845	1,721	1,208	513
Total women	**100.0%**	**59.3%**	**56.6%**	**42.7%**	**14.0%**
No children under age 18	100.0	54.0	51.6	38.8	12.9
With children under age 18	100.0	71.0	67.8	51.3	16.4
Children aged 6 to 17, none younger	100.0	77.2	74.3	57.8	16.5
Children under age 6	100.0	63.3	59.6	43.2	16.4
Children under age 3	100.0	59.2	55.4	39.2	16.3
Children under age 1	100.0	55.1	51.4	36.1	15.3

Source: Bureau of Labor Statistics, Employment Characteristics of Families, Internet site http://www.bls.gov/news.release/famee.toc.htm

Table 4.3 Child Care Arrangements among Preschoolers, 2005

(percent distribution of children aged 0 to 6 and not yet in kindergarten by type of care arrangement and family characteristics, 2005)

| | | any nonparental care | | | |
| | | | home-based care | | |
	parental care only	total	by relative	by nonrelative	center-based program
Total children	**39.2%**	**60.8%**	**22.3%**	**13.9%**	**36.1%**
Aged 0 to 2	49.3	50.7	22.0	15.6	19.6
Aged 3 to 6	23.6	73.7	22.7	11.7	57.1
Race and Hispanic origin					
Asian	43.5	56.5	21.3	9.0	37.0
Black, non-Hispanic	30.1	69.9	27.7	10.2	43.9
Hispanic	50.5	49.5	21.2	10.4	25.2
White, non-Hispanic	37.2	62.8	21.0	17.0	37.8
Mother's employment status					
35 hours or more per week	14.7	85.3	31.8	23.3	47.6
Less than 35 hours per week	30.3	69.7	30.5	18.0	37.8
Not in labor force	66.1	33.9	7.8	3.6	25.8
Family type					
Two parents	42.9	57.1	18.8	14.1	34.4
One parent	24.9	75.1	36.0	13.4	42.3
Educational attainment of mother					
Less than high school	63.7	36.3	16.1	5.5	18.9
High school graduate	44.4	55.6	24.1	9.9	30.7
Some college or associate's degree	36.5	63.5	25.8	14.5	35.2
Bachelor's degree or more	30.5	69.5	19.1	19.2	45.8
Region					
Northeast	38.3	61.7	21.0	15.1	37.9
Midwest	38.0	62.0	22.3	11.1	38.8
South	36.7	63.3	23.8	18.8	33.5
West	43.9	56.1	21.8	12.6	33.1

Note: Numbers may not sum to total in nonparental care because multiple types of child care arrangements may be used.
Source: National Center for Education Statistics, America's Children: Key National Indicators of Children's Well-Being, 2007, Internet site http://childstats.gov/americaschildren/tables.asp

Table 4.4 Before- and After-School Arrangements and Activities among School-Aged Children, 2005

(percent of children in kindergarten through eighth grade participating in child care and before- and after-school activities, by grade, 2005)

	kindergarten through third grade	fourth through eighth grade
Care arrangements		
Parental care only	53.1%	46.9%
Nonparental care	46.9	53.1
Home-based care	23.6	18.1
Center-based care	24.4	19.0
Activities used for supervision	5.2	9.0
Self-care	2.6	22.2
Activities		
Any activity	46.2	53.7
Sports	31.8	39.3
Religious activities	19.4	24.9
Arts	17.2	21.5
Scouts	12.9	10.1
Academic activities	4.7	9.7
Community services	4.2	12.7
Clubs	3.2	8.7

Note: Percentages will not sum to total because children may participate in more than one activity.
Source: National Center for Education Statistics, America's Children: Key National Indicators of Children's Well-Being, 2007, Internet site http://childstats.gov/americaschildren/tables.asp

Fact #5

Incomes Are Falling for Families with Children

The children's market is gasping for breath as spiraling costs and shrinking wages suck the oxygen out of family budgets. This is a new turn of events for American families, who have enjoyed generally rising incomes for decades. Between 1974 and 2000, the median income of households with children grew by 22 percent, after adjusting for inflation. But between 2000 and 2006, family income fell 4 percent. The median income of married couples with children peaked in 2001; female-headed family income peaked in 2000; male-headed family income peaked in 1999. The prospects for getting back on track are dimming.

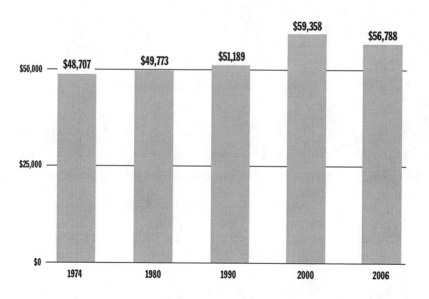

Family incomes peaked in 2000

(median income of families with children, 1974 to 2006; in 2006 dollars)

Behind the decline in family incomes are fundamental economic changes resulting from globalization and the Internet. The median earnings of American men who work full-time peaked years ago in 1978. Family incomes continued to rise until 2000 only because a growing share of women went to work. But women's labor force participation is probably close to its maximum, and women's median earnings peaked in 2002. Now, families face rising costs with little chance of an increase in wages.

Some families are struggling more than others. Married couples have much higher incomes than single-parent families, largely because most couples have two incomes.

The median income of married couples with children is nearly three times the median income of single-parent families

(median income of families with children by family type, 2006)

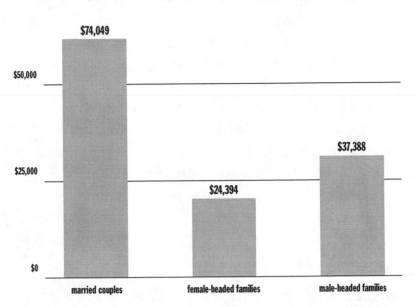

Marriage makes a big difference to the economic status of men and women, boosting their household incomes from below to above average. Consequently, children who live with mom *and* dad will be more affluent than those living with mom *or* dad.

Asian and non-Hispanic white families have much higher incomes than black or Hispanic families. Asian median family income, in fact, is more than twice as high as black or Hispanic median family income.

Among families with children, Asians have the highest incomes

(median income of families with children, by race and Hispanic origin of householder, 2006)

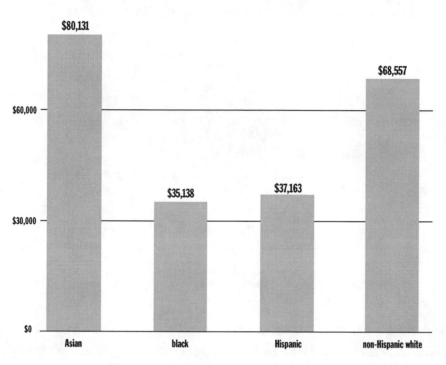

Asian family incomes are far above average because Asians are highly educated and the great majority are two-income couples. Hispanic family incomes are below average because most Hispanics have little education, which results in low earnings. Black families have low incomes because most are headed by single parents. Since a growing share of children in the United States are Hispanic or black, the typical child lives in a low- to middle-income family.

The Census Bureau examined the income distribution of the nation's 74 million children in a 2004 analysis. The results show that a substantial 34 percent of children live in families with monthly incomes below $3,000 (annual income of $36,000 or less). This figure exceeds the 32 percent of children living in families with monthly incomes of $6,000 or more (annual income of $72,000 or more).

More than one-third of children live in a family with a monthly income of less than $3,000

(percent distribution of children under age 18 by monthly family income, 2004)

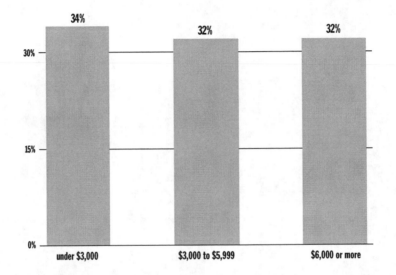

Although there is variation in the incomes of families with children, all are in the same boat as the economy shifts under their feet. Every family has to cope with the rapidly rising cost of necessities—such as food, gasoline, and health insurance. Every family must also cope with slow or no wage growth.

CONSIDER THESE POINTS

■ Although the children's market has an upscale segment, most children live in families with modest or even meager incomes.

■ Parents' number-one concern is providing financial stability for their children. This stability is threatened by economic change, and parents are looking for help.

Table 5.1 Median Income of Families with Children, 1974 to 2006

(median income of total households and families with related children under age 18 by family type, 1974 to 2006; percent change in median income for selected years; in 2006 dollars; bold denotes income peak)

	total households	families with children			
		total	married-couple	female-headed	male-headed
2006	$48,201	$56,788	$74,049	$24,394	$37,388
2005	47,845	56,985	73,176	23,889	37,767
2004	47,323	56,389	72,389	24,986	38,853
2003	47,488	56,284	72,813	24,803	34,985
2002	47,530	56,991	73,295	25,370	36,036
2001	48,091	58,070	**74,256**	25,051	36,366
2000	49,163	**59,358**	73,909	**25,658**	38,032
1999	**49,244**	57,843	72,620	24,113	**39,185**
1998	48,034	56,134	70,439	22,741	38,132
1997	46,350	54,542	68,132	21,614	35,908
1996	45,416	52,445	66,242	20,971	33,911
1995	44,764	52,568	65,643	21,327	35,456
1994	43,405	51,020	63,557	20,048	32,411
1993	42,926	49,739	62,584	18,511	30,706
1992	43,135	50,030	62,222	18,681	31,281
1991	43,492	50,515	61,377	18,785	34,895
1990	44,778	51,189	61,702	19,578	37,702
1989	45,382	52,529	62,792	20,377	38,867
1988	44,587	51,826	61,958	19,446	37,455
1987	44,247	52,359	61,847	19,296	39,386
1986	43,699	51,432	60,268	17,834	–
1985	42,205	49,508	57,807	18,005	–
1984	41,430	48,616	56,819	18,054	–
1983	40,182	46,799	54,189	17,610	–
1982	40,465	47,246	54,454	17,957	–
1981	40,573	48,340	55,774	19,591	–
1980	41,258	49,773	56,625	19,718	–
1979	42,606	52,281	58,539	21,216	–
1978	42,725	51,591	57,887	19,953	–
1977	40,187	49,111	55,211	19,252	–
1976	39,961	48,916	54,256	18,717	–
1975	39,302	47,433	52,379	18,269	–
1974	40,383	48,707	53,763	18,816	–
Percent change					
2000 to 2006	–2.0%	–4.3%	0.2%	–4.9%	–1.7%
1974 to 2000	21.7	21.9	37.5	36.4	–

Note: "–" means data are not available. Number of households with related children is larger than the number of households with own children shown in earlier tables because of differences in definitions.
Source: Bureau of the Census, Current Population Surveys, Annual Social and Economic Supplement, Internet site http://www .census.gov/hhes/www/income/histinc/incfamdet.html; calculations by New Strategist

Table 5.2 Income of Families with Children by Family Type, 2006

(number and percent distribution of families with related children under age 18 at home by income and family type, 2006; families in thousands in 2007)

	total	married-couple	female-headed	male-headed
Total families with children	**39,780**	**27,317**	**9,894**	**2,569**
Under $10,000	2,640	403	2,012	222
$10,000 to $19,999	3,502	1,053	2,129	319
$20,000 to $29,999	3,737	1,601	1,733	405
$30,000 to $39,999	3,956	2,236	1,306	411
$40,000 to $49,999	3,635	2,445	879	311
$50,000 to $59,999	3,277	2,466	571	240
$60,000 to $69,999	2,947	2,400	385	163
$70,000 to $79,999	2,717	2,326	271	120
$80,000 to $89,999	2,216	1,988	154	73
$90,000 to $99,999	1,830	1,666	102	61
$100,000 or more	9,325	8,732	350	243
Median income	$56,788	$74,049	$24,394	$37,388

Percent distribution

	total	married-couple	female-headed	male-headed
Total families with children	**100.0%**	**100.0%**	**100.0%**	**100.0%**
Under $10,000	6.6	1.5	20.3	8.6
$10,000 to $19,999	8.8	3.9	21.5	12.4
$20,000 to $29,999	9.4	5.9	17.5	15.8
$30,000 to $39,999	9.9	8.2	13.2	16.0
$40,000 to $49,999	9.1	9.0	8.9	12.1
$50,000 to $59,999	8.2	9.0	5.8	9.3
$60,000 to $69,999	7.4	8.8	3.9	6.3
$70,000 to $79,999	6.8	8.5	2.7	4.7
$80,000 to $89,999	5.6	7.3	1.6	2.8
$90,000 to $99,999	4.6	6.1	1.0	2.4
$100,000 or more	23.4	32.0	3.5	9.5

Note: Number of households with related children is larger than the number of households with own children shown in earlier tables because of differences in definitions.
Source: Bureau of the Census, 2007 Current Population Survey Annual Social and Economic Supplement, Internet site http://pubdb3.census.gov/macro/032007/faminc/toc.htm; calculations by New Strategist

Table 5.3 Income of Families with Children by Race and Hispanic Origin, 2006

(number and percent distribution of families with related children under age 18 at home by income and race and Hispanic origin of householder, 2006; families in thousands in 2007)

	total	Asian	black	Hispanic	non-Hispanic white
Total families with children	**39,780**	**1,872**	**5,998**	**6,982**	**24,666**
Under $10,000	2,640	65	883	551	1,136
$10,000 to $19,999	3,502	107	929	1,031	1,412
$20,000 to $29,999	3,737	114	782	1,073	1,744
$30,000 to $39,999	3,956	115	719	1,027	2,076
$40,000 to $49,999	3,635	152	577	795	2,093
$50,000 to $59,999	3,277	130	437	592	2,089
$60,000 to $69,999	2,947	137	367	419	1,989
$70,000 to $79,999	2,717	114	273	358	1,933
$80,000 to $89,999	2,216	123	207	227	1,650
$90,000 to $99,999	1,830	83	160	201	1,368
$100,000 or more	9,325	733	664	709	7,174
Median income	$56,788	$80,131	$35,138	$37,163	$68,557

Percent distribution

	total	Asian	black	Hispanic	non-Hispanic white
Total families with children	**100.0%**	**100.0%**	**100.0%**	**100.0%**	**100.0%**
Under $10,000	6.6	3.5	14.7	7.9	4.6
$10,000 to $19,999	8.8	5.7	15.5	14.8	5.7
$20,000 to $29,999	9.4	6.1	13.0	15.4	7.1
$30,000 to $39,999	9.9	6.1	12.0	14.7	8.4
$40,000 to $49,999	9.1	8.1	9.6	11.4	8.5
$50,000 to $59,999	8.2	6.9	7.3	8.5	8.5
$60,000 to $69,999	7.4	7.3	6.1	6.0	8.1
$70,000 to $79,999	6.8	6.1	4.6	5.1	7.8
$80,000 to $89,999	5.6	6.6	3.5	3.3	6.7
$90,000 to $99,999	4.6	4.4	2.7	2.9	5.5
$100,000 or more	23.4	39.2	11.1	10.2	29.1

Note: Asians and blacks are those who identify themselves as being of the race alone or the race in combination with other races. Non-Hispanic whites are those who identify themselves as being white alone and not Hispanic. Hispanics may be of any race. Numbers will not add to total because not all races are shown. Number of households with related children is larger than the number of households with own children shown in earlier tables because of differences in definitions.
Source: Bureau of the Census, 2007 Current Population Survey Annual Social and Economic Supplement, Internet site http://pubdb3.census.gov/macro/032007/faminc/toc.htm; calculations by New Strategist

Table 5.4 Children by Monthly Family Income, 2004

(number and percent distribution of total children under age 18 by monthly family income and age of child, 2004; numbers in thousands)

	total	under 6	6 to 11	12 to 17
Total children	**73,170**	**23,901**	**24,007**	**25,262**
Under $1,500	10,809	3,897	3,643	3,269
$1,500 to $2,999	14,432	4,761	4,856	4,815
$3,000 to $4,499	12,744	4,076	4,126	4,542
$4,500 to $5,999	10,567	3,236	3,635	3,696
$6,000 or more	23,235	7,341	7,285	8,609
Percent distribution				
Total children	**100.0%**	**100.0%**	**100.0%**	**100.0%**
Under $1,500	14.8	16.3	15.2	12.9
$1,500 to $2,999	19.7	19.9	20.2	19.1
$3,000 to $4,499	17.4	17.1	17.2	18.0
$4,500 to $5,999	14.4	13.5	15.1	14.6
$6,000 or more	31.8	30.7	30.3	34.1

Note: Numbers will not add to total because income was not reported for some children.
Source: Bureau of the Census, A Child's Day: 2004 (Selected Indicators of Child Well-Being), Detailed Tables, Internet site http://www.census.gov/population/www/socdemo/2004_detailedtables.html; calculations by New Strategist

Fact #6

Families with Children Are the Biggest Spenders

The problem facing parents is this: at no other time of life are costs greater than when children need to be fed, clothed, and housed—not to mention educated. This explains why married couples with children spend more money than any other household type. In 2006, their spending was 41 percent above average.

Married couples with children spend more than average

(average anual spending of total households and married couples with children, 2006)

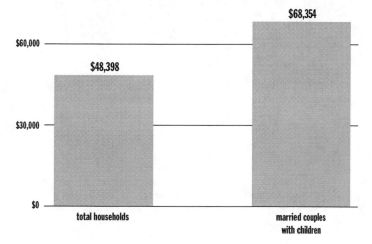

Although married couples with children spend more than any other household type, much of their spending is devoted to the necessities required by larger households. Many have little discretionary income. Single-parent families typically have no discretionary income.

On cereal and milk, married couples with children spend 54 to 56 percent more than the average household. On new cars and trucks, their spending is 66 percent above average. On mortgage interest, they spend 75 percent more than the average household.

Married couples with children spend much more than the average household on new cars and trucks

(average annual spending of married couples with children at home indexed to the annual spending of the average household, for selected goods and services, 2006)

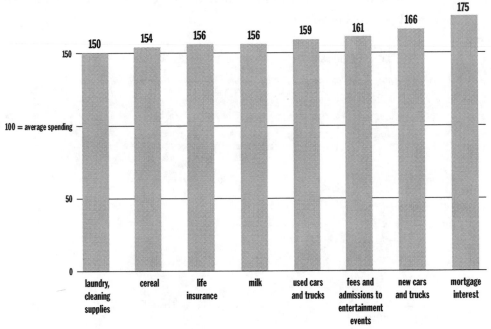

The spending patterns of married couples differ depending on the age of their children. Those with preschoolers spend more than seven times the average on household personal services (mostly day care). They spend more than five times the average on clothes for infants. Married couples with school-aged children are the biggest spenders on entertainment, particularly fees and admission to entertainment events. Married couples with adult children at home (and often younger children as well) are the biggest spenders on telephone services, vehicle purchases, and gasoline.

To keep up with these costs, both mother and father are at work in most married-couple families. Single-parent families face even greater economic difficulties, raising children on only one income. This explains why single-parent families spend less than the average household on most items. Nevertheless, single parents spend more than average on such items as cereal, nonalcoholic beverages, rent, telephone service, household personal services (day care), children's clothes, and shoes.

CONSIDER THESE POINTS

■ As families tighten their belts, competitive pricing is critical to staying afloat in the children's market.

■ Opportunities in the children's market will grow fastest among families in the middle and lower end of the socioeconomic scale because those segments are expanding more rapidly than the upper end.

■ The high end of the children's market is significantly influenced by the spending of grandparents, most of whom have more discretionary dollars than today's parents.

Table 6.1 Average Annual Spending of Households with Children, 2006

(average annual spending of total households and households with children, by type of household, 2006)

		married couples with children				single parent, children <18
Average annual spending	total households	total	oldest child under 6	oldest child 6 to 17	oldest child 18 or older	
	$48,398	$68,354	$63,416	$69,157	$70,234	$35,491
FOOD	6,111	8,864	7,121	9,211	9,356	5,139
Food at home	3,417	5,032	4,053	5,088	5,578	3,046
Cereals and bakery products	446	674	509	708	715	412
Cereals and cereal products	143	220	167	230	235	152
Bakery products	304	454	342	478	480	259
Meats, poultry, fish, and eggs	797	1,152	788	1,150	1,401	725
Beef	236	335	245	324	416	205
Pork	157	222	146	219	278	142
Other meats	105	161	101	166	192	102
Poultry	141	214	154	216	250	137
Fish and seafood	122	173	108	176	211	108
Eggs	37	48	34	49	54	31
Dairy products	368	556	518	573	548	315
Fresh milk and cream	140	219	216	230	199	135
Other dairy products	228	337	302	343	349	180
Fruits and vegetables	592	869	737	868	957	446
Fresh fruits	195	288	260	286	312	132
Fresh vegetables	193	289	216	286	344	123
Processed fruits	109	159	155	157	164	99
Processed vegetables	95	132	106	139	137	92
Other food at home	1,212	1,782	1,500	1,788	1,957	1,148
Sugar and other sweets	125	176	131	180	200	97
Fats and oils	86	121	88	119	147	69
Miscellaneous foods	627	955	863	958	1,011	611
Nonalcoholic beverages	332	470	362	474	536	346
Food prepared by household on trips	43	59	55	58	63	25
Food away from home	2,694	3,831	3,068	4,123	3,777	2,093
ALCOHOLIC BEVERAGES	497	500	476	506	502	232
HOUSING	16,366	22,502	24,837	22,728	20,522	13,840
Shelter	9,673	12,957	14,092	13,493	11,221	8,055
Owned dwellings*	6,516	10,260	11,083	10,681	8,943	3,926
Mortgage interest and charges	3,753	6,568	7,644	6,872	5,287	2,414
Property taxes	1,649	2,371	2,324	2,474	2,217	909
Maintenance, repairs, insurance, other expenses	1,115	1,321	1,114	1,335	1,438	603
Rented dwellings	2,590	1,939	2,483	2,100	1,281	3,938
Other lodging	567	758	527	713	997	190

(continued)

	total households	married couples with children				single parent, children <18
		total	oldest child under 6	oldest child 6 to 17	oldest child 18 or older	
Utilities, fuels, public services	**$3,397**	**$4,432**	**$3,731**	**$4,488**	**$4,811**	**$3,331**
Natural gas	509	665	606	674	690	492
Electricity	1,266	1,620	1,355	1,645	1,755	1,282
Fuel oil and other fuels	138	176	133	191	179	60
Telephone services	1,087	1,438	1,195	1,425	1,627	1,152
Water and other public services	397	533	442	553	559	345
Household services	**948**	**1,793**	**3,485**	**1,585**	**1,013**	**969**
Personal services	393	1,122	2,829	869	410	642
Other household services	555	671	656	715	603	327
Housekeeping supplies	**640**	**926**	**754**	**942**	**1,011**	**423**
Laundry and cleaning supplies	151	226	203	221	253	150
Other household products	330	510	379	534	547	177
Postage and stationery	159	190	172	187	210	96
Household furnishings, equipment	**1,708**	**2,392**	**2,775**	**2,219**	**2,466**	**1,063**
Household textiles	154	193	192	151	278	101
Furniture	463	666	964	629	529	305
Floor coverings	48	69	68	72	64	11
Major appliances	241	357	368	312	435	113
Small appliances, misc. housewares	109	135	102	122	184	69
Misc. household equipment	693	972	1,082	933	976	465
APPAREL AND SERVICES	**1,874**	**2,805**	**2,666**	**2,852**	**2,828**	**1,863**
Men and boys	**444**	**735**	**589**	**781**	**755**	**329**
Men, aged 16 or older	353	518	436	467	677	115
Boys, aged 2 to 15	91	217	153	314	78	214
Women and girls	**751**	**1,127**	**936**	**1,150**	**1,222**	**812**
Women, aged 16 or older	629	829	748	734	1,078	533
Girls, aged 2 to 15	122	298	188	417	144	279
Children under age 2	**96**	**188**	**552**	**122**	**71**	**110**
Footwear	**304**	**445**	**327**	**471**	**472**	**447**
Other apparel products and services	**280**	**310**	**263**	**328**	**309**	**164**
TRANSPORTATION	**8,508**	**12,787**	**11,188**	**12,769**	**13,909**	**5,504**
Vehicle purchases	**3,421**	**5,553**	**5,211**	**5,587**	**5,725**	**1,917**
Cars and trucks, new	1,798	2,978	3,065	3,078	2,738	553
Cars and trucks, used	1,568	2,492	2,131	2,414	2,876	1,353
Gasoline and motor oil	**2,227**	**3,246**	**2,609**	**3,246**	**3,680**	**1,697**
Other vehicle expenses	**2,355**	**3,381**	**2,909**	**3,326**	**3,800**	**1,628**
Vehicle finance charges	298	497	519	494	486	193
Maintenance and repairs	688	958	646	995	1,102	467
Vehicle insurance	886	1,235	947	1,137	1,606	666
Vehicle rental, leases, licenses, other charges	482	691	797	699	605	303
Public transportation	**505**	**608**	**459**	**610**	**705**	**261**

(continued)

	total households	married couples with children				single parent, children <18
		total	oldest child under 6	oldest child 6 to 17	oldest child 18 or older	
HEALTH CARE	$2,766	$3,133	$2,726	$3,038	$3,583	$1,306
Health insurance	1,465	1,623	1,449	1,570	1,839	644
Medical services	670	871	855	864	894	383
Drugs	514	492	336	448	679	209
Medical supplies	117	146	86	156	171	70
ENTERTAINMENT	2,376	3,378	2,879	3,738	3,064	1,859
Fees and admissions	606	976	573	1,229	797	402
Audio and visual equipment, services	906	1,195	1,081	1,241	1,186	819
Pets, toys, hobbies, playground equipment	412	573	591	579	551	288
Other entertainment supplies, services	451	635	633	689	531	350
PERSONAL CARE PRODUCTS AND SERVICES	585	813	747	783	921	460
READING	117	137	105	144	146	63
EDUCATION	888	1,769	570	1,633	2,826	754
TOBACCO PRODUCTS AND SMOKING SUPPLIES	327	311	215	319	361	259
MISCELLANEOUS	846	944	774	964	1,026	644
CASH CONTRIBUTIONS	1,869	2,083	1,347	2,116	2,525	733
PERSONAL INSURANCE AND PENSIONS	5,270	8,330	7,766	8,356	8,666	2,835
Life and other personal insurance	322	501	363	522	557	150
Pensions and Social Security	4,948	7,829	7,403	7,834	8,109	2,686
PERSONAL TAXES	2,432	3,287	3,524	2,986	3,665	220
Federal income taxes	1,711	2,261	2,477	2,037	2,518	(118)
State and local income taxes	519	794	854	736	858	214
Other taxes	202	231	194	213	289	124
GIFTS FOR PEOPLE IN OTHER HOUSEHOLDS**	1,154	1,286	904	1,438	1,287	484

* This figure does not include the amount paid for mortgage principle, which is considered an asset.
** Spending on gifts is also included in the preceding product and service categories. Food spending, for example, includes the amount spent on gifts of food.
Source: Bureau of Labor Statistics, 2006 Consumer Expenditure Survey, Internet site http://www.bls.gov/cex/home.htm

Table 6.2 Indexed Average Annual Spending of Households with Children, 2006

(indexed average annual spending of households with children, by type of household, 2006)

	total households	married couples with children				single parent, children <18
		total	oldest child under 6	oldest child 6 to 17	oldest child 18 or older	
Indexed average annual spending	100	141	131	143	145	73
FOOD	100	145	117	151	153	84
Food at home	100	147	119	149	163	89
Cereals and bakery products	100	151	114	159	160	92
Cereals and cereal products	100	154	117	161	164	106
Bakery products	100	149	113	157	158	85
Meats, poultry, fish, and eggs	100	145	99	144	176	91
Beef	100	142	104	137	176	87
Pork	100	141	93	139	177	90
Other meats	100	153	96	158	183	97
Poultry	100	152	109	153	177	97
Fish and seafood	100	142	89	144	173	89
Eggs	100	130	92	132	146	84
Dairy products	100	151	141	156	149	86
Fresh milk and cream	100	156	154	164	142	96
Other dairy products	100	148	132	150	153	79
Fruits and vegetables	100	147	124	147	162	75
Fresh fruits	100	148	133	147	160	68
Fresh vegetables	100	150	112	148	178	64
Processed fruits	100	146	142	144	150	91
Processed vegetables	100	139	112	146	144	97
Other food at home	100	147	124	148	161	95
Sugar and other sweets	100	141	105	144	160	78
Fats and oils	100	141	102	138	171	80
Miscellaneous foods	100	152	138	153	161	97
Nonalcoholic beverages	100	142	109	143	161	104
Food prepared by household on trips	100	137	128	135	147	58
Food away from home	100	142	114	153	140	78
ALCOHOLIC BEVERAGES	100	101	96	102	101	47
HOUSING	100	137	152	139	125	85
Shelter	100	134	146	139	116	83
Owned dwellings*	100	157	170	164	137	60
Mortgage interest and charges	100	175	204	183	141	64
Property taxes	100	144	141	150	134	55
Maintenance, repairs, insurance, other expenses	100	118	100	120	129	54
Rented dwellings	100	75	96	81	49	152
Other lodging	100	134	93	126	176	34

(continued)

	total households	married couples with children				single parent, children <18
		total	oldest child under 6	oldest child 6 to 17	oldest child 18 or older	
Utilities, fuels, public services	**100**	**130**	**110**	**132**	**142**	**98**
Natural gas	100	131	119	132	136	97
Electricity	100	128	107	130	139	101
Fuel oil and other fuels	100	128	96	138	130	43
Telephone services	100	132	110	131	150	106
Water and other public services	100	134	111	139	141	87
Household services	**100**	**189**	**368**	**167**	**107**	**102**
Personal services	100	285	720	221	104	163
Other household services	100	121	118	129	109	59
Housekeeping supplies	**100**	**145**	**118**	**147**	**158**	**66**
Laundry and cleaning supplies	100	150	134	146	168	99
Other household products	100	155	115	162	166	54
Postage and stationery	100	119	108	118	132	60
Household furnishings and equipment	**100**	**140**	**162**	**130**	**144**	**62**
Household textiles	100	125	125	98	181	66
Furniture	100	144	208	136	114	66
Floor coverings	100	144	142	150	133	23
Major appliances	100	148	153	129	180	47
Small appliances, misc. housewares	100	124	94	112	169	63
Misc. household equipment	100	140	156	135	141	67
APPAREL AND SERVICES	**100**	**150**	**142**	**152**	**151**	**99**
Men and boys	**100**	**166**	**133**	**176**	**170**	**74**
Men, aged 16 or older	100	147	124	132	192	33
Boys, aged 2 to 15	100	238	168	345	86	235
Women and girls	**100**	**150**	**125**	**153**	**163**	**108**
Women, aged 16 or older	100	132	119	117	171	85
Girls, aged 2 to 15	100	244	154	342	118	229
Children under age 2	**100**	**196**	**575**	**127**	**74**	**115**
Footwear	**100**	**146**	**108**	**155**	**155**	**147**
Other apparel products and services	**100**	**111**	**94**	**117**	**110**	**59**
TRANSPORTATION	**100**	**150**	**131**	**150**	**163**	**65**
Vehicle purchases	**100**	**162**	**152**	**163**	**167**	**56**
Cars and trucks, new	100	166	170	171	152	31
Cars and trucks, used	100	159	136	154	183	86
Gasoline and motor oil	**100**	**146**	**117**	**146**	**165**	**76**
Other vehicle expenses	**100**	**144**	**124**	**141**	**161**	**69**
Vehicle finance charges	100	167	174	166	163	65
Maintenance and repairs	100	139	94	145	160	68
Vehicle insurance	100	139	107	128	181	75
Vehicle rental, leases, licenses, other charges	100	143	165	145	126	63
Public transportation	**100**	**120**	**91**	**121**	**140**	**52**

(continued)

	total households	married couples with children				single parent, children <18
		total	oldest child under 6	oldest child 6 to 17	oldest child 18 or older	
HEALTH CARE	100	113	99	110	130	47
Health insurance	100	111	99	107	126	44
Medical services	100	130	128	129	133	57
Drugs	100	96	65	87	132	41
Medical supplies	100	125	74	133	146	60
ENTERTAINMENT	100	142	121	157	129	78
Fees and admissions	100	161	95	203	132	66
Audio and visual equipment, services	100	132	119	137	131	90
Pets, toys, hobbies, playground equipment	100	139	143	141	134	70
Other entertainment supplies, services	100	141	140	153	118	78
PERSONAL CARE PRODUCTS AND SERVICES	100	139	128	134	157	79
READING	100	117	90	123	125	54
EDUCATION	100	199	64	184	318	85
TOBACCO PRODUCTS AND SMOKING SUPPLIES	100	95	66	98	110	79
MISCELLANEOUS	100	112	91	114	121	76
CASH CONTRIBUTIONS	100	111	72	113	135	39
PERSONAL INSURANCE AND PENSIONS	100	158	147	159	164	54
Life and other personal insurance	100	156	113	162	173	47
Pensions and Social Security	100	158	150	158	164	54
PERSONAL TAXES	100	135	145	123	151	9
Federal income taxes	100	132	145	119	147	(7)
State and local income taxes	100	153	165	142	165	41
Other taxes	100	114	96	105	143	61
GIFTS FOR PEOPLE IN OTHER HOUSEHOLDS**	100	111	78	125	112	42

* This figure does not include the amount paid for mortgage principle, which is considered an asset.
** Spending on gifts is also included in the preceding product and service categories. Food spending, for example, includes the amount spent on gifts of food. Index definition: an index of 100 is the average for all households; an index of 132 means that spending by the household type is 32 percent above the average for all households; an index of 68 indicates spending that is 32 percent below the average for all households.
Source: Bureau of Labor Statistics, 2006 Consumer Expenditure Survey, Internet site http://www.bls.gov/cex/home.htm; calculations by New Strategist

Fact #7

Many Children Do Not Live with Both Parents

In the business of selling to parents and children, the target market can range from some of the most affluent households in the nation (dual-income married couples) to some of the poorest (female-headed families). Unfortunately, the fastest growing segments of the children's market today are families who are financially strapped. That is because the number of children living with only their mother is growing faster than the number of children living with both parents.

The percentage of children living with only their mother has more than doubled over the past few decades

(percentage of children under age 18 living with only their mother, 1970 and 2007)

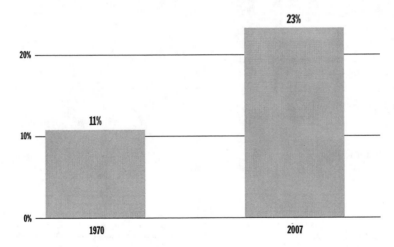

In 2007, only 71 percent of children lived with both parents (including unmarried parents)—down from 85 percent in 1970. The percentage of children living with only their mother climbed from 11 to 23 percent during those years. Although there has been much discussion in the media about the number of children who live with a grandparent, in fact most children who live with a grandparent also live with a parent.

There are enormous differences in children's living arrangements by race and Hispanic origin. Only 40 percent of black children live with both parents compared with 86 percent of Asian, 79 percent of non-Hispanic white, and 70 percent of Hispanic children.

Children's living arrangements vary greatly by race and Hispanic origin

(percent of children under age 18 living with both parents, by race and Hispanic origin, 2007)

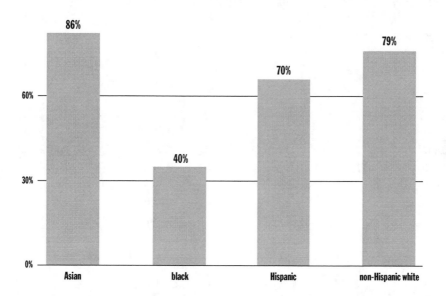

Children's economic well-being depends on their living arrangement. Those living with both parents are better off because both parents work. Those living with single mothers are not as well off because most of their households have only one earner. Since a large percentage of today's children live in a single-parent family, many children have relatively low family incomes.

CONSIDER THESE POINTS

■ Time is in short supply regardless of family type. Consequently, many purchasing decisions are impulsive rather than planned.

■ Although the number of children living with only their father has grown rapidly over the past few decades, 90 percent of children still live with mom. Mothers continue to be the point person for most purchasing decisions in the children's market.

Table 7.1 Living Arrangements of Children by Race and Hispanic Origin, 1970 to 2007

(number and percent distribution of children under age 18 by race, Hispanic origin, and living arrangement, 1970 to 2007; numbers in thousands)

	total	both parents	mother only	father only	other relatives	nonrelatives only
Total children						
2007 (new)	73,746	70.7%	22.6%	3.2%	2.7%	0.7%
2007	73,746	67.8	24.2	4.5	2.7	0.7
2000	72,012	69.1	22.4	4.2	3.0	1.2
1990	64,137	72.5	21.6	3.1	2.2	0.5
1980	63,427	76.7	18.0	1.7	3.1	0.6
1970	69,162	85.2	10.8	1.1	2.2	0.7
Black						
2007 (new)	12,375	40.2	49.7	3.5	5.8	0.8
2007	12,375	37.1	51.3	4.9	5.8	0.8
2000	11,412	37.6	49.0	4.2	7.7	1.5
1990	10,018	37.7	51.2	3.5	6.5	1.0
1980	9,375	42.2	43.9	1.9	10.7	1.3
1970	9,422	58.5	29.5	2.3	8.7	1.0
Hispanic						
2007 (new)	15,113	69.9	24.5	2.1	2.9	0.7
2007	15,113	65.6	26.8	4.1	2.9	0.7
2000	11,613	65.1	25.1	4.4	3.7	1.7
1990	7,174	66.8	27.1	2.9	2.5	0.8
1980	5,459	75.4	19.6	1.5	3.4	0.1
1970	4,006	77.7	–	–	–	–
White						
2007 (new)	56,223	76.8	17.3	3.2	2.1	0.7
2007	56,223	73.9	18.9	4.4	2.1	0.7
2000	56,455	75.3	17.3	4.3	2.0	1.1
1990	51,390	79.0	16.2	3.0	1.4	0.4
1980	52,242	82.7	13.5	1.6	1.7	0.5
1970	58,791	89.5	7.8	0.9	1.2	0.6

Note: The "new" 2007 numbers include children living with two parents who are not married to one another, the first time the Census Bureau has analyzed the data in this way. "–" means data are not available.
Source: Bureau of the Census, Families and Living Arrangements, Historical Time Series, Internet site http://www.census .gov/population/www/socdemo/hh-fam.html; calculations by New Strategist

Table 7.2 Living Arrangements of Children by Race and Hispanic Origin, 2007

(number and percent distribution of children under age 18 by living arrangement and race and Hispanic origin, 2007; numbers in thousands)

	total	Asian	black	Hispanic	non-Hispanic white
Total children	**73,746**	**3,569**	**12,375**	**15,113**	**42,261**
Living with both parents	52,153	3,072	4,979	10,557	33,228
Living with mother only	16,658	350	6,146	3,700	6,455
Living with father only	2,388	65	432	317	1,533
Living with neither parent	2,545	80	818	537	1,046
Percent distribution by living arrangement					
Total children	**100.0%**	**100.0%**	**100.0%**	**100.0%**	**100.0%**
Living with both parents	70.7	86.1	40.2	69.9	78.6
Living with mother only	22.6	9.8	49.7	24.5	15.3
Living with father only	3.2	1.8	3.5	2.1	3.6
Living with neither parent	3.5	2.2	6.6	3.6	2.5
Percent distribution by race and Hispanic origin					
Total children	**100.0%**	**4.8%**	**16.8%**	**20.5%**	**57.3%**
Living with both parents	100.0	5.9	9.5	20.2	63.7
Living with mother only	100.0	2.1	36.9	22.2	38.8
Living with father only	100.0	2.7	18.1	13.3	64.2
Living with neither parent	100.0	3.1	32.1	21.1	41.1

Note: Asians and blacks are those who identify themselves as being of the race alone or as being of the race in combination with other races. Non-Hispanic whites are those who identify themselves as being white alone and not Hispanic. Hispanics may be of any race. Numbers will not add to total because not all races are shown.
Source: Bureau of the Census, America's Families and Living Arrangements: 2007, Internet site http://www.census.gov/ population/www/socdemo/hh-fam/cps2007.html; calculations by New Strategist

Table 7.3 Children Living with Grandparents, 1970 to 2007

(number and percent distribution of children living in the home of a grandparent by presence of parent, 1970 to 2007; numbers in thousands)

	total children	total	living in grandparents' home				without parents present
			with parents present				
			total	both parents	mother only	father only	
2007	73,746	4,013	2,706	709	1,793	204	1,307
2000	72,012	3,842	2,483	531	1,732	220	1,359
1990	64,137	3,155	2,221	467	1,563	191	935
1980	63,369	2,306	1,318	310	922	86	988
1970	69,276	2,214	1,258	363	817	78	957

Percent distribution by living arrangement

2007	100.0%	5.4%	3.7%	1.0%	2.4%	0.3%	1.8%
2000	100.0	5.3	3.4	0.7	2.4	0.3	1.9
1990	100.0	4.9	3.5	0.7	2.4	0.3	1.5
1980	100.0	3.6	2.1	0.5	1.5	0.1	1.6
1970	100.0	3.2	1.8	0.5	1.2	0.1	1.4

Percent distribution of children living with a grandparent by presence of parent in the home

2007	–	100.0%	67.4%	17.7%	44.7%	5.1%	32.6%
2000	–	100.0	64.6	13.8	45.1	5.7	35.4
1990	–	100.0	70.4	14.8	49.5	6.1	29.6
1980	–	100.0	57.2	13.4	40.0	3.7	42.8
1970	–	100.0	56.8	16.4	36.9	3.5	43.2

Note: "–" means not applicable.
Source: Bureau of the Census, Families and Living Arrangements, Historical Time Series, Internet site http://www.census
.gov/population/www/socdemo/hh-fam.html; calculations by New Strategist

Fact #8

The Children's Market Is Multiracial

As if 74 million children were not fragmented enough by age, income, and living arrangement, another complication is their racial and ethnic diversity. Just 57 percent of Americans under age 18 are non-Hispanic white, while 43 percent are Asian, black, or Hispanic.

Children are much more diverse than older Americans

(percent of people under age 18 and aged 65 or older who are minorities, 2007)

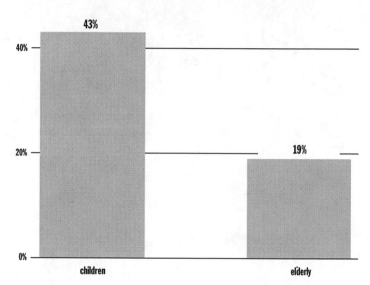

The racial and ethnic differences between young and old create tensions in many communities. The priorities of non-Hispanic whites, who are older, differ from those of blacks and Hispanics, who are younger.

Hispanics are the largest minority among children, accounting for 21 percent of the population under age 18. Blacks are a slightly smaller 17 percent, while Asians account for just 5 percent of the nation's children. Younger children are more diverse than older children, thanks to the growing Hispanic population.

One in four children under age 5 is Hispanic

(percent distributiuon of people under age 5 by race and Hispanic origin, 2007)

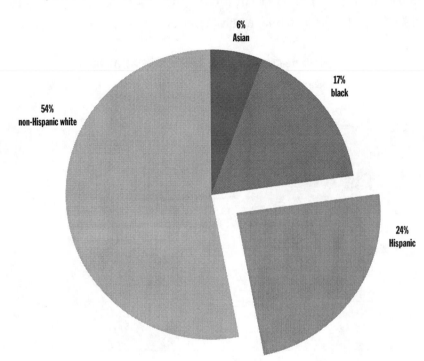

Children will continue to grow more diverse during the next few decades. Eventually, non-Hispanic whites will become a minority and no single racial or ethnic group will be in the majority.

Because blacks and Hispanics account for such a large share of children, black and Hispanic families account for a large share of spending in the children's market. In fact, the combined black and Hispanic share of spending on many products and services is substantial. They account for 32 percent of spending on shoes, for example.

Black and Hispanic households control nearly one-third of spending on footwear

(share of total household spending on selected products and services controlled by black and Hispanic households, 2006)

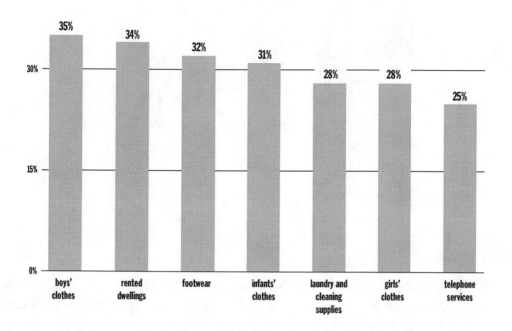

Black and Hispanic households control more than one-fourth of household spending on many foods such as beef, pork, poultry, fish, and eggs. They also control more than one-fourth of spending on telephone services. They control at least 30 percent of the market for boys' clothes, infants' clothes, and footwear.

The children's market is not only racially diverse, but also linguistically diverse. A substantial 15 percent of school-aged children speak Spanish at home. Most also speak English "very well," however, easing the challenge of marketing to this population.

**Most children who speak Spanish at home are bilingual—
many of their parents are not**

(percent of people who speak Spanish at home who also speak English "very well," by age, 2006)

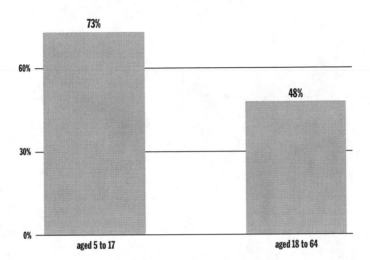

CONSIDER THESE POINTS

■ Multicultural and multiracial may be a discussion point for marketers, corporate executives, and politicians, many of whom still inhabit a nearly all-white world. But to the nation's children, multicultural and multiracial is the norm.

■ English will work most of the time when communicating with children from Spanish-speaking households. It often will not work when communicating with their parents and grandparents.

Table 8.1 Population by Age, 2007

(number and percent distribution of people by age, 2007; numbers in thousands)

	number	percent distribution
Five-year age groups		
Total people	**301,621**	**100.0%**
Under age 5	20,724	6.9
Aged 5 to 9	19,850	6.6
Aged 10 to 14	20,314	6.7
Aged 15 to 19	21,474	7.1
Aged 20 to 24	21,032	7.0
Aged 25 to 29	21,058	7.0
Aged 30 to 34	19,533	6.5
Aged 35 to 39	21,176	7.0
Aged 40 to 44	21,985	7.3
Aged 45 to 49	22,861	7.6
Aged 50 to 54	21,013	7.0
Aged 55 to 59	18,236	6.0
Aged 60 to 64	14,476	4.8
Aged 65 to 69	10,752	3.6
Aged 70 to 74	8,600	2.9
Aged 75 to 79	7,325	2.4
Aged 80 to 84	5,699	1.9
Aged 85 or older	5,512	1.8
Selected age groups		
Total people	**301,621**	**100.0**
Under age 18	73,902	24.5
Under age 5	20,724	6.9
Aged 5 to 13	35,971	11.9
Aged 14 to 17	17,207	5.7
Aged 18 to 64	189,831	62.9
Aged 18 to 24	29,492	9.8
Aged 25 to 44	83,752	27.8
Aged 45 to 64	76,587	25.4
Aged 65 or older	37,888	12.6

Source: Bureau of the Census, Population Estimates, Internet site http://www.census.gov/popest/national/asrh/; calculations by New Strategist

Table 8.2 Population by Age, Race, and Hispanic Origin, 2007

(number of people by age, race, and Hispanic origin, 2007; numbers in thousands)

	total	Asian	black	Hispanic	non-Hispanic white
Five-year age groups					
Total people	**301,621**	**15,165**	**40,744**	**45,504**	**199,092**
Under age 5	20,724	1,170	3,567	4,916	11,175
Aged 5 to 9	19,850	1,048	3,334	4,219	11,255
Aged 10 to 14	20,314	1,027	3,431	3,969	11,866
Aged 15 to 19	21,474	1,011	3,620	3,746	13,006
Aged 20 to 24	21,032	1,036	3,260	3,690	12,930
Aged 25 to 29	21,058	1,223	3,094	4,176	12,497
Aged 30 to 34	19,533	1,372	2,701	3,993	11,425
Aged 35 to 39	21,176	1,374	2,827	3,642	13,272
Aged 40 to 44	21,985	1,196	2,894	3,200	14,597
Aged 45 to 49	22,861	1,080	2,860	2,675	16,109
Aged 50 to 54	21,013	957	2,479	2,075	15,363
Aged 55 to 59	18,236	800	2,002	1,569	13,736
Aged 60 to 64	14,476	567	1,388	1,122	11,294
Aged 65 to 69	10,752	425	1,035	809	8,408
Aged 70 to 74	8,600	327	814	621	6,786
Aged 75 to 79	7,325	245	603	479	5,959
Aged 80 to 84	5,699	166	431	322	4,751
Aged 85 or older	5,512	141	403	280	4,663
Selected age groups					
Total people	**301,621**	**15,165**	**40,744**	**45,504**	**199,092**
Under age 18	73,902	3,853	12,558	15,419	42,113
Under age 5	20,724	1,170	3,567	4,916	11,175
Aged 5 to 13	35,971	1,873	6,040	7,402	20,652
Aged 14 to 17	17,207	811	2,951	3,101	10,286
Aged 18 to 64	189,831	10,008	24,899	27,573	126,412
Aged 18 to 24	29,492	1,438	4,655	5,122	18,119
Aged 25 to 44	83,752	5,165	11,515	15,010	51,792
Aged 45 to 64	76,587	3,405	8,729	7,441	56,501
Aged 65 or older	37,888	1,304	3,287	2,512	30,567

Note: Numbers by race and Hispanic origin will not sum to total because Asians and blacks include those who identify themselves as being of the race alone and those who identify themselves as being of the race in combination with other races, Hispanics may be of any race, and not all races are shown. Non-Hispanic whites are those who identify themselves as white alone and not Hispanic.
Source: Bureau of the Census, Population Estimates, Internet site http://www.census.gov/popest/national/asrh/; calculations by New Strategist

Table 8.3 Distribution of Population by Age, Race, and Hispanic Origin, 2007

(percent distribution of people by age, race, and Hispanic origin, 2007; numbers in thousands)

	total	Asian	black	Hispanic	non-Hispanic white
Five-year age groups					
Total people	**100.0%**	**5.0%**	**13.5%**	**15.1%**	**66.0%**
Under age 5	100.0	5.6	17.2	23.7	53.9
Aged 5 to 9	100.0	5.3	16.8	21.3	56.7
Aged 10 to 14	100.0	5.1	16.9	19.5	58.4
Aged 15 to 19	100.0	4.7	16.9	17.4	60.6
Aged 20 to 24	100.0	4.9	15.5	17.5	61.5
Aged 25 to 29	100.0	5.8	14.7	19.8	59.3
Aged 30 to 34	100.0	7.0	13.8	20.4	58.5
Aged 35 to 39	100.0	6.5	13.4	17.2	62.7
Aged 40 to 44	100.0	5.4	13.2	14.6	66.4
Aged 45 to 49	100.0	4.7	12.5	11.7	70.5
Aged 50 to 54	100.0	4.6	11.8	9.9	73.1
Aged 55 to 59	100.0	4.4	11.0	8.6	75.3
Aged 60 to 64	100.0	3.9	9.6	7.8	78.0
Aged 65 to 69	100.0	4.0	9.6	7.5	78.2
Aged 70 to 74	100.0	3.8	9.5	7.2	78.9
Aged 75 to 79	100.0	3.3	8.2	6.5	81.3
Aged 80 to 84	100.0	2.9	7.6	5.7	83.4
Aged 85 or older	100.0	2.5	7.3	5.1	84.6
Selected age groups					
Total people	**100.0%**	**5.0%**	**13.5%**	**15.1%**	**66.0%**
Under age 18	100.0	5.2	17.0	20.9	57.0
Under age 5	100.0	5.6	17.2	23.7	53.9
Aged 5 to 13	100.0	5.2	16.8	20.6	57.4
Aged 14 to 17	100.0	4.7	17.2	18.0	59.8
Aged 18 to 64	100.0	5.3	13.1	14.5	66.6
Aged 18 to 24	100.0	4.9	15.8	17.4	61.4
Aged 25 to 44	100.0	6.2	13.7	17.9	61.8
Aged 45 to 64	100.0	4.4	11.4	9.7	73.8
Aged 65 or older	100.0	3.4	8.7	6.6	80.7

Note: Percentages by race and Hispanic origin will not sum to total because Asians and blacks include those who identify themselves as being of the race alone and those who identify themselves as being of the race in combination with other races, Hispanics may be of any race, and not all races are shown. Non-Hispanic whites are those who identify themselves as white alone and not Hispanic.
Source: Bureau of the Census, Population Estimates, Internet site http://www.census.gov/popest/national/asrh/; calculations by New Strategist

Table 8.4 Spending of Black Households, 2006

(average annual, indexed, and market share of spending by households headed by blacks, 2006)

	total consumer units	black average	black index	black market share
Number of consumer units	118,843	14,265	–	12.0%
Average annual spending of consumer units	$48,398	$34,583	71	8.6
FOOD	**6,111**	**4,530**	**74**	**8.9**
Food at home	**3,417**	**2,796**	**82**	**9.8**
Cereals and bakery products	446	366	82	9.9
Cereals and cereal products	143	133	93	11.2
Bakery products	304	232	76	9.2
Meats, poultry, fish, and eggs	797	845	106	12.7
Beef	236	213	90	10.8
Pork	157	186	118	14.2
Other meats	105	88	84	10.1
Poultry	141	179	127	15.2
Fish and seafood	122	141	116	13.9
Eggs	37	38	103	12.3
Dairy products	368	237	64	7.7
Fresh milk and cream	140	101	72	8.7
Other dairy products	228	135	59	7.1
Fruits and vegetables	592	432	73	8.8
Fresh fruits	195	123	63	7.6
Fresh vegetables	193	120	62	7.5
Processed fruits	109	102	94	11.2
Processed vegetables	95	87	92	11.0
Other food at home	1,212	916	76	9.1
Sugar and other sweets	125	90	72	8.6
Fats and oils	86	73	85	10.2
Miscellaneous foods	627	461	74	8.8
Nonalcoholic beverages	332	278	84	10.1
Food prepared by consumer unit on trips	43	13	30	3.6
Food away from home	**2,694**	**1,735**	**64**	**7.7**
ALCOHOLIC BEVERAGES	**497**	**$210**	**42**	**5.1**
HOUSING	**16,366**	**12,754**	**78**	**9.4**
Shelter	**9,673**	**7,378**	**76**	**9.2**
Owned dwellings*	6,516	3,600	55	6.6
Mortgage interest and charges	3,753	2,378	63	7.6
Property taxes	1,649	753	46	5.5
Maintenance, repair, insurance, other expenses	1,115	469	42	5.0
Rented dwellings	2,590	3,555	137	16.5
Other lodging	567	223	39	4.7

(continued)

	total consumer units	black		
		average	index	market share
Utilities, fuels, public services	$3,397	$3,461	102	12.2%
Natural gas	509	593	117	14.0
Electricity	1,266	1,333	105	12.6
Fuel oil and other fuels	138	39	28	3.4
Telephone services	1,087	1,154	106	12.7
Water and other public services	397	342	86	10.3
Household services	**948**	**545**	**57**	**6.9**
Personal services	393	269	68	8.2
Other household services	555	276	50	6.0
Housekeeping supplies	**640**	**482**	**75**	**9.0**
Laundry and cleaning supplies	151	188	125	14.9
Other household products	330	218	66	7.9
Postage and stationery	159	76	48	5.7
Household furnishings and equipment	**1,708**	**888**	**52**	**6.2**
Household textiles	154	87	56	6.8
Furniture	463	300	65	7.8
Floor coverings	48	10	21	2.5
Major appliances	241	119	49	5.9
Small appliances and miscellaneous housewares	109	52	48	5.7
Miscellaneous household equipment	693	319	46	5.5
APPAREL AND RELATED SERVICES	**1,874**	**1,762**	**94**	**11.3**
Men and boys	**444**	**385**	**87**	**10.4**
Men, aged 16 or older	353	266	75	9.0
Boys, aged 2 to 15	91	120	132	15.8
Women and girls	**751**	**636**	**85**	**10.2**
Women, aged 16 or older	629	529	84	10.1
Girls, aged 2 to 15	122	108	89	10.6
Children under age 2	**96**	**108**	**113**	**13.5**
Footwear	**304**	**391**	**129**	**15.4**
Other apparel products, services	**280**	**241**	**86**	**10.3**
TRANSPORTATION	**8,508**	**6,130**	**72**	**8.6**
Vehicle purchases	**3,421**	**2,362**	**69**	**8.3**
Cars and trucks, new	1,798	1,046	58	7.0
Cars and trucks, used	1,568	1,280	82	9.8
Other vehicles	54	36	67	8.0
Gasoline and motor oil	**2,227**	**1,740**	**78**	**9.4**
Other vehicle expenses	**2,355**	**1,742**	**74**	**8.9**
Vehicle finance charges	298	246	83	9.9
Maintenance and repairs	688	456	66	8.0
Vehicle insurance	886	710	80	9.6
Vehicle rentals, leases, licenses, other charges	482	330	68	8.2
Public transportation	**505**	**286**	**57**	**6.8**

(continued)

	total consumer units	black average	black index	black market share
HEALTH CARE	**$2,766**	**$1,497**	**54**	**6.5%**
Health insurance	1,465	927	63	7.6
Medical services	670	248	37	4.4
Drugs	514	272	53	6.4
Medical supplies	117	49	42	5.0
ENTERTAINMENT	**2,376**	**1,172**	**49**	**5.9**
Fees and admissions	606	192	32	3.8
Audio and visual equipment, services	906	747	82	9.9
Pets, toys, and playground equipment	412	143	35	4.2
Other entertainment products, services	451	91	20	2.4
PERSONAL CARE PRODUCTS AND SERVICES	**585**	**519**	**89**	**10.6**
READING	**117**	**46**	**39**	**4.7**
EDUCATION	**888**	**495**	**56**	**6.7**
TOBACCO PRODUCTS AND SMOKING SUPPLIES	**327**	**187**	**57**	**6.9**
MISCELLANEOUS	**846**	**544**	**64**	**7.7**
CASH CONTRIBUTIONS	**1,869**	**1,384**	**74**	**8.9**
PERSONAL INSURANCE AND PENSIONS	**5,270**	**3,354**	**64**	**7.6**
Life and other personal insurance	322	245	76	9.1
Pensions and Social Security	4,948	3,109	63	7.5
PERSONAL TAXES	**2,432**	**626**	**26**	**3.1**
Federal income taxes	1,711	336	20	2.4
State and local income taxes	519	222	43	5.1
Other taxes	202	69	34	4.1
GIFTS FOR PEOPLE IN OTHER HOUSEHOLDS**	**1,154**	**552**	**48**	**5.7**

* This figure does not include the amount paid for mortgage principle, which is considered an asset.
** Spending on gifts is also included in the preceding product and service categories. Food spending, for example, includes the amount spent on gifts of food
Source: Bureau of Labor Statistics, 2006 Consumer Expenditure Survey, Internet site http://www.bls.gov/cex/; calculations by New Strategist

Table 8.5 Spending of Hispanic Households, 2006

(average annual, indexed, and market share of spending by households headed by Hispanics, 2006)

	total consumer units	Hispanic average	Hispanic index	Hispanic market share
Number of consumer units	118,843	13,664	–	11.5%
Average annual spending of consumer units	$48,398	$43,053	89	10.2
FOOD	6,111	6,170	101	11.6
Food at home	3,417	3,719	109	12.5
Cereals and bakery products	446	427	96	11.0
Cereals and cereal products	143	164	115	13.2
Bakery products	304	263	87	9.9
Meats, poultry, fish, and eggs	797	999	125	14.4
Beef	236	310	131	15.1
Pork	157	197	125	14.4
Other meats	105	104	99	11.4
Poultry	141	185	131	15.1
Fish and seafood	122	146	120	13.8
Eggs	37	58	157	18.0
Dairy products	368	384	104	12.0
Fresh milk and cream	140	176	126	14.5
Other dairy products	228	208	91	10.5
Fruits and vegetables	592	735	124	14.3
Fresh fruits	195	258	132	15.2
Fresh vegetables	193	250	130	14.9
Processed fruits	109	123	113	13.0
Processed vegetables	95	105	111	12.7
Other food at home	1,212	1,173	97	11.1
Sugar and other sweets	125	101	81	9.3
Fats and oils	86	91	106	12.2
Miscellaneous foods	627	582	93	10.7
Nonalcoholic beverages	332	365	110	12.6
Food prepared by consumer unit on trips	43	33	77	8.8
Food away from home	2,694	2,451	91	10.5
ALCOHOLIC BEVERAGES	497	326	66	7.5
HOUSING	16,366	15,412	94	10.8
Shelter	9,673	9,639	100	11.5
Owned dwellings*	6,516	5,355	82	9.4
Mortgage interest and charges	3,753	3,459	92	10.6
Property taxes	1,649	1,181	72	8.2
Maintenance, repair, insurance, other expenses	1,115	715	64	7.4
Rented dwellings	2,590	4,031	156	17.9
Other lodging	567	253	45	5.1

(continued)

	total consumer units	Hispanic		
		average	index	market share
Utilities, fuels, public services	**$3,397**	**$3,224**	**95**	**10.9%**
Natural gas	509	377	74	8.5
Electricity	1,266	1,203	95	10.9
Fuel oil and other fuels	138	40	29	3.3
Telephone services	1,087	1,202	111	12.7
Water and other public services	397	403	102	11.7
Household services	**948**	**661**	**70**	**8.0**
Personal services	393	330	84	9.7
Other household services	555	331	60	6.9
Housekeeping supplies	**640**	**529**	**83**	**9.5**
Laundry and cleaning supplies	151	176	117	13.4
Other household products	330	280	85	9.8
Postage and stationery	159	73	46	5.3
Household furnishings and equipment	**1,708**	**1,359**	**80**	**9.1**
Household textiles	154	154	100	11.5
Furniture	463	424	92	10.5
Floor coverings	48	26	54	6.2
Major appliances	241	205	85	9.8
Small appliances and misc. housewares	109	84	77	8.9
Miscellaneous household equipment	693	465	67	7.7
APPAREL AND RELATED SERVICES	**1,874**	**2,278**	**122**	**14.0**
Men and boys	**444**	**603**	**136**	**15.6**
Men, aged 16 or older	353	450	127	14.7
Boys, aged 2 to 15	91	153	168	19.3
Women and girls	**751**	**844**	**112**	**12.9**
Women, aged 16 or older	629	662	105	12.1
Girls, aged 2 to 15	122	182	149	17.2
Children under age 2	**96**	**143**	**149**	**17.1**
Footwear	**304**	**427**	**140**	**16.1**
Other apparel products, services	**280**	**262**	**94**	**10.8**
TRANSPORTATION	**8,508**	**8,286**	**97**	**11.2**
Vehicle purchases	**3,421**	**3,400**	**99**	**11.4**
Cars and trucks, new	1,798	1,661	92	10.6
Cars and trucks, used	1,568	1,690	108	12.4
Other vehicles	54	50	93	10.6
Gasoline and motor oil	**2,227**	**2,319**	**104**	**12.0**
Other vehicle expenses	**2,355**	**2,152**	**91**	**10.5**
Vehicle finance charges	298	326	109	12.6
Maintenance and repairs	688	610	89	10.2
Vehicle insurance	886	814	92	10.6
Vehicle rentals, leases, licenses, other charges	482	402	83	9.6
Public transportation	**505**	**414**	**82**	**9.4**

(continued)

	total consumer units	Hispanic		
		average	index	market share
HEALTH CARE	$2,766	$1,659	60	6.9%
Health insurance	1,465	780	53	6.1
Medical services	670	504	75	8.6
Drugs	514	305	59	6.8
Medical supplies	117	69	59	6.8
ENTERTAINMENT	2,376	1,568	66	7.6
Fees and admissions	606	401	66	7.6
Audio and visual equipment, services	906	772	85	9.8
Pets, toys, playground equipment	412	207	50	5.8
Other entertainment products, services	451	188	42	4.8
PERSONAL CARE PRODUCTS AND SERVICES	585	537	92	10.6
READING	117	43	37	4.2
EDUCATION	888	633	71	8.2
TOBACCO PRODUCTS AND SMOKING SUPPLIES	327	150	46	5.3
MISCELLANEOUS	846	575	68	7.8
CASH CONTRIBUTIONS	1,869	1,343	72	8.3
PERSONAL INSURANCE AND PENSIONS	5,270	4,074	77	8.9
Life and other personal insurance	322	151	47	5.4
Pensions and Social Security	4,948	3,923	79	9.1
PERSONAL TAXES	2,432	1,034	43	4.9
Federal income taxes	1,711	753	44	5.1
State and local income taxes	519	231	45	5.1
Other taxes	202	50	25	2.8
GIFTS FOR PEOPLE IN OTHER HOUSEHOLDS**	1,154	792	69	7.9

* This figure does not include the amount paid for mortgage principle, which is considered an asset.
** Spending on gifts is also included in the preceding product and service categories. Food spending, for example, includes the amount spent on gifts of food
Source: Bureau of Labor Statistics, 2006 Consumer Expenditure Survey, Internet site http://www.bls.gov/cex/; calculations by New Strategist

Table 8.6 Language Spoken at Home by Age, 2006

(number and percent distribution of people aged 5 or older by language spoken at home and ability to speak English, by age, 2006; numbers in thousands)

	number	percent distribution
Language spoken at home		
Total population	**279,013**	**100.0%**
Speak only English at home	224,154	80.3
Speak Spanish at home	34,045	12.2
Speak other language at home	20,813	7.5
Aged 5 to 17	**53,379**	**100.0**
Speak only English at home	42,518	79.7
Speak Spanish at home	7,805	14.6
Speak other language at home	3,057	5.7
Aged 18 to 64	**188,442**	**100.0**
Speak only English at home	149,626	79.4
Speak Spanish at home	23,984	12.7
Speak other language at home	14,832	7.9
Aged 65 or older	**37,191**	**100.0**
Speak only English at home	32,011	86.1
Speak Spanish at home	2,256	6.1
Speak other language at home	2,924	7.9

	number	percent of speakers
Speak English less than "very well"		
Total population		
Spanish speakers	16,119	47.3%
Other language speakers	8,094	38.9
Aged 5 to 17		
Spanish speakers	2,076	26.6
Other language speakers	690	22.6
Aged 18 to 64		
Spanish speakers	12,591	52.5
Other language speakers	5,838	39.4
Aged 65 or older		
Spanish speakers	1,451	64.3
Other language speakers	1,565	53.5

Source: Bureau of the Census, 2006 American Community Survey, Internet site http://factfinder.census.gov/home/saff/main .html?_lang=en; calculations by New Strategist

Fact #9

The Children's Market Is Local

The children's market is much more diverse in some states than in others. Among children in California, fully 69 percent are American Indian, Asian, black, or Hispanic. In Vermont, the figure is just 6 percent.

The largest states are some of the most diverse

(minority share of population under age 18 in the five most populous states, 2006)

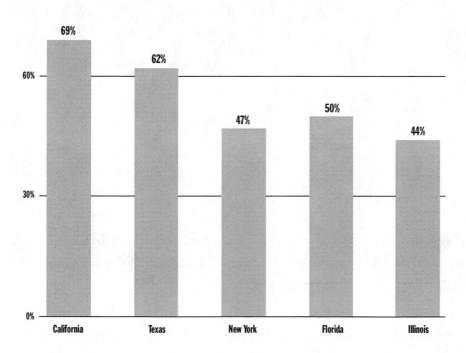

Because the country's most populous states are also the most diverse, the multicultural influence of the growing Hispanic and black populations extends even into the states that are overwhelmingly non-Hispanic white.

In the nation's public school system, ten states have minority majorities. In California, fully 69 percent of public school students are (in order of size) Hispanic, Asian, black, or American Indian.

In ten states, more than half of public school students are minorities

(minority share of public school students in states in which minorities are the majority of students, 2005)

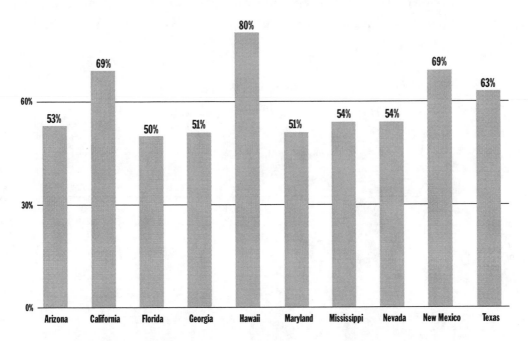

And that is not the end of the diversity story. In five states—Arizona, California, Nevada, New Mexico, and Texas—more than one in four school-aged children speak Spanish at home. The figure exceeds 10 percent in 13 states.

Race, Hispanic origin, and language are not the only things segmenting children geographically. In Mississippi, married couples account for only 59 percent of families with children. In Utah, the figure is 80 percent. In Connecticut, only 9 percent of families with children are in poverty. In West Virginia, the figure is 21 percent.

The racial diversity of children differs dramatically by state. So do children's living arrangements and economic status. If your customers are children and their parents, you need to know the local demographics to respond appropriately to their wants and needs.

CONSIDER THIS POINT

■ The best way to track the demographics of children at the local level is through the Census Bureau's American Community Survey. See Appendix 2 for more about this survey.

Table 9.1 Number of Children by State, Race, and Hispanic Origin, 2006

(number of people under age 18 by race and Hispanic origin, by state, 2006)

	total	Asian	black	Hispanic	non-Hispanic white
Total under age 18	**73,765,143**	**2,905,528**	**10,921,949**	**14,955,592**	**42,249,752**
Alabama	1,115,668	11,821	349,941	40,426	693,180
Alaska	179,687	6,819	5,397	13,071	102,239
Arizona	1,626,855	32,130	62,232	675,313	730,217
Arkansas	693,036	7,651	136,061	52,558	473,840
California	9,531,046	950,214	640,147	4,598,703	2,954,713
Colorado	1,169,643	31,049	50,057	324,406	722,177
Connecticut	817,866	27,936	99,072	127,566	544,479
Delaware	203,736	6,355	51,657	20,042	119,834
District of Columbia	114,830	2,260	80,784	11,072	18,008
Florida	4,018,644	86,945	852,284	957,137	2,017,601
Georgia	2,452,225	60,523	844,373	247,379	1,247,843
Hawaii	297,233	83,986	6,767	35,490	52,857
Idaho	394,315	3,196	–	54,652	319,318
Illinois	3,216,387	117,096	580,840	657,714	1,791,135
Indiana	1,579,597	18,921	174,866	106,867	1,237,978
Iowa	714,520	11,252	23,426	44,730	612,150
Kansas	694,667	14,055	44,854	88,423	515,408
Kentucky	1,000,341	8,594	89,516	27,004	847,109
Louisiana	1,088,997	12,865	420,903	30,957	600,810
Maine	281,872	3,640	6,119	4,304	259,976
Maryland	1,362,132	60,550	446,219	105,681	701,424
Massachusetts	1,448,477	70,021	116,144	167,128	1,050,950
Michigan	2,477,421	57,781	433,495	138,227	1,763,173
Minnesota	1,257,930	56,624	82,332	73,094	987,058
Mississippi	758,927	4,483	341,684	13,942	386,127
Missouri	1,422,429	21,746	202,465	57,964	1,091,479
Montana	218,098	1,930	–	7,486	179,719
Nebraska	445,410	7,057	24,040	51,463	346,153
Nevada	634,447	30,471	54,965	222,751	290,741
New Hampshire	297,678	7,020	3,933	9,836	271,231

(continued)

	total	Asian	black	Hispanic	non-Hispanic white
New Jersey	2,089,653	154,131	334,782	397,242	1,164,692
New Mexico	510,350	5,557	12,954	269,427	155,326
New York	4,513,489	279,750	834,501	913,346	2,403,698
North Carolina	2,155,019	42,426	535,708	214,793	1,280,257
North Dakota	143,612	–	–	2,985	122,513
Ohio	2,772,776	39,835	411,968	91,408	2,146,409
Oklahoma	895,186	14,116	79,067	93,226	560,056
Oregon	857,617	32,407	19,783	142,494	614,131
Pennsylvania	2,807,534	66,270	380,701	187,125	2,104,029
Rhode Island	237,447	7,214	16,538	42,141	162,120
South Carolina	1,038,866	10,994	347,823	48,584	600,960
South Dakota	193,977	–	–	5,804	151,369
Tennessee	1,447,050	20,364	304,005	67,237	1,018,434
Texas	6,502,854	194,280	812,389	2,923,046	2,456,574
Utah	792,172	11,642	8,326	109,642	626,978
Vermont	133,904	1,615	–	1,978	125,826
Virginia	1,805,553	80,654	406,216	147,499	1,103,876
Washington	1,527,876	90,620	65,170	221,991	1,036,334
West Virginia	390,221	1,834	12,245	5,298	360,029
Wisconsin	1,314,943	36,828	115,200	93,402	1,025,515
Wyoming	120,930	–	–	11,538	101,699

Note: Numbers will not add to total because each race includes only those who identified themselves as being of the race alone, not all races are shown, and Hispanics may be of any race. Non-Hispanic whites are those who identified themselves as being white alone and not Hispanic. "–" means sample is too small to make a reliable estimate.
Source: Bureau of the Census, 2006 American Community Survey, Internet site http://factfinder.census.gov/home/saff/main .html?_lang=en; calculations by New Strategist

(distribution of people under age 18 by race and Hispanic origin, by state, 2006)

	total	Asian	black	Hispanic	non-Hispanic white
Total under age 18	**100.0%**	**3.9%**	**14.8%**	**20.3%**	**57.3%**
Alabama	100.0	1.1	31.4	3.6	62.1
Alaska	100.0	3.8	3.0	7.3	56.9
Arizona	100.0	2.0	3.8	41.5	44.9
Arkansas	100.0	1.1	19.6	7.6	68.4
California	100.0	10.0	6.7	48.2	31.0
Colorado	100.0	2.7	4.3	27.7	61.7
Connecticut	100.0	3.4	12.1	15.6	66.6
Delaware	100.0	3.1	25.4	9.8	58.8
District of Columbia	100.0	2.0	70.4	9.6	15.7
Florida	100.0	2.2	21.2	23.8	50.2
Georgia	100.0	2.5	34.4	10.1	50.9
Hawaii	100.0	28.3	2.3	11.9	17.8
Idaho	100.0	0.8	–	13.9	81.0
Illinois	100.0	3.6	18.1	20.4	55.7
Indiana	100.0	1.2	11.1	6.8	78.4
Iowa	100.0	1.6	3.3	6.3	85.7
Kansas	100.0	2.0	6.5	12.7	74.2
Kentucky	100.0	0.9	8.9	2.7	84.7
Louisana	100.0	1.2	38.7	2.8	55.2
Maine	100.0	1.3	2.2	1.5	92.2
Maryland	100.0	4.4	32.8	7.8	51.5
Massachusetts	100.0	4.8	8.0	11.5	72.6
Michigan	100.0	2.3	17.5	5.6	71.2
Minnesota	100.0	4.5	6.5	5.8	78.5
Mississippi	100.0	0.6	45.0	1.8	50.9
Missouri	100.0	1.5	14.2	4.1	76.7
Montana	100.0	0.9	–	3.4	82.4
Nebraska	100.0	1.6	5.4	11.6	77.7
Nevada	100.0	4.8	8.7	35.1	45.8
New Hampshire	100.0	2.4	1.3	3.3	91.1

(continued)

	total	Asian	black	Hispanic	non-Hispanic white
New Jersey	100.0%	7.4%	16.0%	19.0%	55.7%
New Mexico	100.0	1.1	2.5	52.8	30.4
New York	100.0	6.2	18.5	20.2	53.3
North Carolina	100.0	2.0	24.9	10.0	59.4
North Dakota	100.0	–	–	2.1	85.3
Ohio	100.0	1.4	14.9	3.3	77.4
Oklahoma	100.0	1.6	8.8	10.4	62.6
Oregon	100.0	3.8	2.3	16.6	71.6
Pennsylvania	100.0	2.4	13.6	6.7	74.9
Rhode Island	100.0	3.0	7.0	17.7	68.3
South Carolina	100.0	1.1	33.5	4.7	57.8
South Dakota	100.0	–	–	3.0	78.0
Tennessee	100.0	1.4	21.0	4.6	70.4
Texas	100.0	3.0	12.5	45.0	37.8
Utah	100.0	1.5	1.1	13.8	79.1
Vermont	100.0	1.2	–	1.5	94.0
Virginia	100.0	4.5	22.5	8.2	61.1
Washington	100.0	5.9	4.3	14.5	67.8
West Virginia	100.0	0.5	3.1	1.4	92.3
Wisconsin	100.0	2.8	8.8	7.1	78.0
Wyoming	100.0	–	–	9.5	84.1

Note: Percentages will not add to total because each race includes only those who identified themselves as being of the race alone, not all races are shown, and Hispanics may be of any race. Non-Hispanic whites are those who identified themselves as being white alone and not Hispanic. "–" means sample is too small to make a reliable estimate.
Source: Bureau of the Census, 2006 American Community Survey, Internet site http://factfinder.census.gov/home/saff/main .html?_lang=en; calculations by New Strategist

Table 9.3 Enrollment in Public Elementary and Secondary Schools by State, Race, and Hispanic Origin, 2005

(percent distribution of students enrolled in public elementary and secondary schools by state, race, and Hispanic origin, 2005)

	total	minority students					non-Hispanic white
		total	Am. Indian	Asian	black	Hispanic	
Total public school children	**100.0%**	**42.9%**	**1.2%**	**4.6%**	**17.2%**	**19.8%**	**57.1%**
Alabama	100.0	40.6	0.8	1.0	36.0	2.8	59.4
Alaska	100.0	42.3	26.6	6.9	4.6	4.2	57.7
Arizona	100.0	52.8	6.2	2.5	5.2	39.0	47.2
Arkansas	100.0	31.8	0.7	1.4	23.0	6.8	68.2
California	100.0	69.0	0.8	11.7	8.0	48.5	31.0
Colorado	100.0	37.5	1.2	3.3	6.0	27.1	62.5
Connecticut	100.0	33.0	0.4	3.6	13.7	15.4	67.0
Delaware	100.0	44.9	0.3	2.8	32.5	9.2	55.1
District of Columbia	100.0	95.5	0.1	1.4	83.3	10.6	4.5
Florida	100.0	50.4	0.3	2.2	23.9	23.9	49.6
Georgia	100.0	50.8	0.1	2.8	39.2	8.7	49.2
Hawaii	100.0	80.2	0.6	72.8	2.4	4.5	19.8
Idaho	100.0	17.0	1.6	1.6	1.0	12.8	83.0
Illinois	100.0	43.6	0.2	3.8	20.6	19.0	56.4
Indiana	100.0	19.7	0.3	1.2	12.5	5.7	80.3
Iowa	100.0	13.4	0.6	1.9	5.1	5.8	86.6
Kansas	100.0	24.6	1.5	2.4	8.6	12.1	75.4
Kentucky	100.0	13.7	0.2	0.9	10.6	2.1	86.3
Louisiana	100.0	48.5	0.8	1.3	44.4	2.1	51.5
Maine	100.0	4.9	0.5	1.4	2.0	0.9	95.1
Maryland	100.0	51.4	0.4	5.2	38.1	7.6	48.6
Massachusetts	100.0	26.5	0.3	4.7	8.4	13.1	73.5
Michigan	100.0	28.1	1.0	2.4	20.3	4.4	71.9
Minnesota	100.0	21.7	2.1	5.7	8.5	5.4	78.3
Mississippi	100.0	53.5	0.2	0.8	51.2	1.4	46.5
Missouri	100.0	23.4	0.4	1.6	18.2	3.2	76.6
Montana	100.0	15.7	11.3	1.1	0.9	2.4	84.3
Nebraska	100.0	22.5	1.7	1.8	7.6	11.5	77.5

(continued)

	total	minority students					non-Hispanic white
		total	Am. Indian	Asian	black	Hispanic	
Nevada	100.0%	53.6%	1.6%	7.3%	11.1%	33.6%	46.4%
New Hampshire	100.0	6.7	0.3	1.9	1.7	2.8	93.3
New Jersey	100.0	43.5	0.2	7.5	17.6	18.2	56.5
New Mexico	100.0	68.9	11.1	1.3	2.5	54.0	31.1
New York	100.0	47.3	0.5	6.9	19.8	20.1	52.7
North Carolina	100.0	43.4	1.4	2.1	31.5	8.4	56.6
North Dakota	100.0	12.8	8.6	0.9	1.5	1.7	87.2
Ohio	100.0	21.0	0.1	1.4	17.1	2.4	79.0
Oklahoma	100.0	40.4	18.9	1.7	10.9	8.9	59.6
Oregon	100.0	26.4	2.4	4.9	3.2	15.9	73.6
Pennsylvania	100.0	25.2	0.1	2.5	16.2	6.4	74.8
Rhode Island	100.0	29.6	0.6	3.1	8.6	17.3	70.4
South Carolina	100.0	46.0	0.3	1.3	40.3	4.0	54.0
South Dakota	100.0	15.0	10.5	1.0	1.6	2.0	85.0
Tennessee	100.0	30.5	0.2	1.4	25.1	3.8	69.5
Texas	100.0	63.5	0.3	3.1	14.7	45.3	36.5
Utah	100.0	18.2	1.5	3.1	1.3	12.3	81.8
Vermont	100.0	4.5	0.4	1.6	1.5	1.0	95.5
Virginia	100.0	40.2	0.3	5.2	27.0	7.7	59.8
Washington	100.0	30.2	2.7	8.1	5.7	13.6	69.8
West Virginia	100.0	6.4	0.1	0.6	5.0	0.7	93.6
Wisconsin	100.0	22.2	1.5	3.6	10.5	6.7	77.8
Wyoming	100.0	15.1	3.5	1.1	1.5	9.0	84.9

Source: National Center for Education Statistics, Digest of Education Statistics: 2007, Internet site http://nces.ed.gov/programs/digest/d07/tables_2.asp#Ch2Sub1

Table 9.4 Children Who Speak Spanish at Home, by State, 2006

(total number of people aged 5 to 17, and number and percent who speak Spanish at home, by state, 2006)

		speak Spanish at home	
	total population	number	percent
Total aged 5 to 17	**53,379,370**	**7,804,711**	**14.6%**
Alabama	821,941	25,435	3.1
Alaska	132,206	4,179	3.2
Arizona	1,147,710	309,152	26.9
Arkansas	498,295	29,280	5.9
California	6,858,380	2,401,517	35.0
Colorado	830,648	125,433	15.1
Connecticut	615,795	66,056	10.7
Delaware	146,645	12,489	8.5
District of Columbia	79,850	8,538	10.7
Florida	2,901,014	570,329	19.7
Georgia	1,753,290	142,185	8.1
Hawaii	210,054	2,279	1.1
Idaho	281,949	27,222	9.7
Illinois	2,327,049	367,211	15.8
Indiana	1,146,017	63,042	5.5
Iowa	523,393	28,190	5.4
Kansas	499,965	42,288	8.5
Kentucky	723,377	16,838	2.3
Louisiana	787,799	19,252	2.4
Maine	211,645	2,985	1.4
Maryland	993,631	67,413	6.8
Massachusetts	1,060,858	93,691	8.8
Michigan	1,838,182	73,165	4.0
Minnesota	910,526	43,021	4.7
Mississippi	552,838	9,611	1.7
Missouri	1,031,714	30,895	3.0
Montana	160,521	2,930	1.8
Nebraska	317,103	27,120	8.6
Nevada	451,010	116,730	25.9

(continued)

		speak Spanish at home	
	total population	number	percent
New Hampshire	224,198	4,987	2.2%
New Jersey	1,529,781	221,433	14.5
New Mexico	368,618	97,464	26.4
New York	3,292,479	512,724	15.6
North Carolina	1,552,286	124,921	8.0
North Dakota	104,518	2,714	2.6
Ohio	2,036,601	52,776	2.6
Oklahoma	643,133	43,538	6.8
Oregon	627,661	76,156	12.1
Pennsylvania	2,083,084	106,668	5.1
Rhode Island	175,649	25,071	14.3
South Carolina	754,158	33,165	4.4
South Dakota	140,276	3,885	2.8
Tennessee	1,048,044	38,027	3.6
Texas	4,580,627	1,415,059	30.9
Utah	545,005	53,425	9.8
Vermont	100,890	1,568	1.6
Virginia	1,302,062	87,093	6.7
Washington	1,121,060	111,330	9.9
West Virginia	285,792	5,713	2.0
Wisconsin	963,241	54,703	5.7
Wyoming	86,802	3,815	4.4

Source: Bureau of the Census, 2006 American Community Survey, Internet site http://www.census.gov/acs/www/; calculations by New Strategist

Fact #10

Parental Aspirations Are Key

The complex demographics of the children's market can make it exceedingly difficult to target. Fortunately, one factor unites the market: the hopes and dreams of parents. Regardless of age, race, income, family type, or geography, parents want their children to succeed. Thus, it is an easy task to determine which messages will resonate with parents—the ones that feed their aspirations.

Both mothers and fathers are heavily invested in their children and will do almost anything to ensure their success. Government surveys document this obsession. Ask new fathers whether they would rather buy something for themselves or for their child, and the two-thirds majority strongly agree that they would rather buy something for their child, according to the National Center for Education Statistics.

New fathers are focused on family

(percent of resident fathers with children aged 9 months who report doing selected activities "all the time," 2001–02)

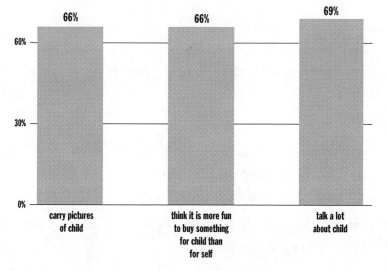

Parents are willing—even happy—to sacrifice their own wants and needs for their children. As family finances tighten, parents will try to maintain spending on their children while they cut expenses elsewhere.

Ask parents whether they want their child to go to college, and nine out of ten say yes—a proportion that hardly varies by race, income, education, or any other child or family characteristic. These aspirations explain why the college market has expanded so much over the past few years. Families are fighting for their children's success, and they have become convinced that college is the surest route to prosperity.

Most parents have lofty aspirations for their children

(percent of parents who want their child to graduate from college, by family income level, 2004)

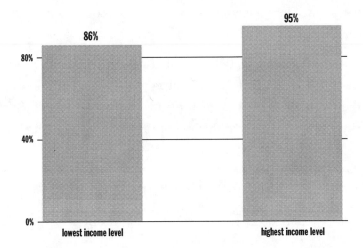

The key to the children's market is helping parents achieve their ultimate goal—to see their children become happy and successful adults. Parents almost universally believe that the rewards of having children are worth the costs. You won't go wrong by helping them confirm that belief.

CONSIDER THESE POINTS

■ Because parents want their children to be happy, they can be pushovers when the kids request a snack, a toy, or an electronic gadget. But with family budgets increasingly tight, parents are struggling with these purchase decisions more than ever.

■ The gap between what parents want for their children and what they can realistically do for them is growing. Help them bridge that gap.

Table 10.1 Attitudes of Fathers, 2001–02

(percentage of resident fathers with children aged 9 months by attitude toward child, 2001–02)

	percent
Fathers' rating of himself as a father	
A very good father	49%
A better than average father	30
An average father	17
Has some trouble being a father	2
Not very good at being a father	0
Father talks a lot about the child to friends and family	
All of the time	69
Some of the time	29
Rarely	2
Never	0
Father carries pictures of the child with him wherever he goes	
All of the time	66
Some of the time	16
Rarely	9
Never	9
Father often finds himself thinking about the child	
All of the time	74
Some of the time	25
Rarely	1
Never	0
Father thinks holding and cuddling the child is fun	
All of the time	85
Some of the time	15
Rarely	0
Never	0

(continued)

	percent
Father thinks it's more fun to get something new for the child than for himself	
All of the time	66%
Some of the time	32
Rarely	2
Never	0
A father should be as heavily involved as the mother in the care of the child	
Strongly agree	54
Agree	38
Disagree	8
Strongly disagree	0
All things considered, fatherhood is a highly rewarding experience	
Strongly agree	84
Agree	15
Disagree	1
Strongly disagree	0

Source: National Center for Education Statistics, Early Childhood Longitudinal Study, Birth Cohort (ECLS-B), Internet site http://nces.ed.gov/pubsearch/pubsinfo.asp?pubid=2006002

Table 10.2 Educational Expectations of Parents, 2004

(percent of children whose parents want them to graduate from college, by demographic characteristic of child and parent, 2004)

	percent of children whose parents want them to graduate from college
Total children	**90.6%**
Sex of child	
Females	91.5
Males	89.7
Race and Hispanic origin of child	
Asian	95.1
Black	90.4
Hispanic	88.7
Non-Hispanic white	91.2
Education of parent	
Less than high school	80.6
High school graduate	86.6
Some college	93.6
Vocational or associate's degree	92.0
Bachelor's degree	96.6
Advanced degree	97.3
Monthly family income	
Under $1,500	86.0
$1,500 to $2,999	87.5
$3,000 to $4,499	89.1
$4,500 to $5,999	91.8
$6,000 and over	95.1
Homeownership status	
Owns home	91.8
Rents home	88.1
Region of residence	
Northeast	92.2
Midwest	88.6
South	90.9
West	90.7

Source: Bureau of the Census, A Child's Day: 2004, Detailed Tables, Internet site http://www.census.gov/population/www/socdemo/2004_detailedtables.html

Table 10.3 Attitude toward the Rewards of Parenthood, 2002

"The rewards of being a parent are worth it,
despite the cost and the work it takes."

(percent of people aged 15 to 44 who agree with statement, by selected characteristics and sex, 2002)

	percent agreeing	
	men	women
Total aged 15 to 44	**93.8%**	**94.2%**
Aged 15 to 24	91.4	93.4
Aged 25 to 29	95.2	93.9
Aged 30 to 44	94.9	94.9
Marital status		
Currently married	97.6	96.0
First marriage	97.6	96.8
Second or later marriage	97.9	92.4
Currently cohabiting	91.0	92.6
Never married, not cohabiting	90.4	92.3
Formerly married, not cohabiting	94.4	94.7
Number of children		
No children	90.1	91.1
One or more children	97.9	96.5
Race and Hispanic origin		
Black, non-Hispanic	92.4	93.8
Hispanic	93.8	93.7
White, non-Hispanic	94.0	94.7
Education		
Not a high school graduate	94.4	93.5
High school graduate or GED	94.7	94.0
Some college, no degree	95.3	95.4
Bachelor's degree or more	94.1	95.1
Current religion		
No religion	88.4	90.4
Fundamentalist Protestant	96.2	98.2
Other Protestant	95.1	95.1
Catholic	94.8	94.4
Other religion	94.7	92.8
Importance of religion		
Very important	95.1	95.3
Somewhat important	95.6	95.1
Not important	89.9	90.3

Source: National Center for Health Statistics, Fertility, Contraception, and Fatherhood: Data on Men and Women from Cycle 6 of the 2002 National Survey of Family Growth, Vital and Health Statistics, Series 23, No. 26, 2006; Internet site http://www.cdc .gov/nchs/nsfg.htm

Appendix 1. Population by State, Age, Race, and Hispanic Origin, 2006

(number and percent distribution of people by state, age, race, and Hispanic origin, 2006)

	total	Asian	black	Hispanic	non-Hispanic white	total	Asian	black	Hispanic	non-Hispanic white
Alabama	**4,599,030**	**45,882**	**1,209,321**	**111,432**	**3,171,700**	**100.0%**	**1.0%**	**26.3%**	**2.4%**	**69.0%**
Under age 18	1,115,668	11,821	349,941	40,426	693,180	100.0	1.1	31.4	3.6	62.1
Under age 5	293,727	3,017	86,995	15,746	182,777	100.0	1.0	29.6	5.4	62.2
Aged 5 to 9	305,444	4,037	93,414	11,800	190,039	100.0	1.3	30.6	3.9	62.2
Aged 10 to 14	317,043	2,998	105,146	7,743	195,393	100.0	0.9	33.2	2.4	61.6
Aged 15 to 17	199,454	1,769	64,386	5,137	124,971	100.0	0.9	32.3	2.6	62.7
Aged 18 to 19	140,746	1,352	47,984	4,642	84,567	100.0	1.0	34.1	3.3	60.1
Aged 20 to 24	319,738	3,861	100,761	12,563	198,206	100.0	1.2	31.5	3.9	62.0
Aged 25 to 29	299,802	3,131	85,693	11,963	195,642	100.0	1.0	28.6	4.0	65.3
Aged 30 to 34	282,654	5,474	75,185	11,315	188,103	100.0	1.9	26.6	4.0	66.5
Aged 35 to 44	649,714	8,869	166,473	17,049	449,188	100.0	1.4	25.6	2.6	69.1
Aged 45 to 54	662,648	5,585	164,946	7,207	475,309	100.0	0.8	24.9	1.1	71.7
Aged 55 to 64	517,689	3,486	107,962	3,633	396,660	100.0	0.7	20.9	0.7	76.6
Aged 65 to 74	325,859	1,405	58,847	1,521	261,116	100.0	0.4	18.1	0.5	80.1
Aged 75 to 84	210,461	693	37,910	556	170,249	100.0	0.3	18.0	0.3	80.9
Aged 85 or older	74,051	205	13,619	557	59,480	100.0	0.3	18.4	0.8	80.3
Alaska	**670,053**	**30,151**	**21,476**	**37,498**	**443,944**	**100.0**	**4.5**	**3.2**	**5.6**	**66.3**
Under age 18	179,687	6,819	5,397	13,071	102,239	100.0	3.8	3.0	7.3	56.9
Under age 5	47,481	1,326	1,160	4,873	26,478	100.0	2.8	2.4	10.3	55.8
Aged 5 to 9	49,376	2,162	1,968	3,998	26,996	100.0	4.4	4.0	8.1	54.7
Aged 10 to 14	48,818	2,230	1,346	2,609	29,313	100.0	4.6	2.8	5.3	60.0
Aged 15 to 17	34,012	1,101	923	1,591	19,452	100.0	3.2	2.7	4.7	57.2
Aged 18 to 19	24,263	1,014	1,347	2,349	12,280	100.0	4.2	5.6	9.7	50.6
Aged 20 to 24	50,473	2,032	2,080	3,798	31,975	100.0	4.0	4.1	7.5	63.4
Aged 25 to 29	49,358	1,731	1,601	3,226	33,999	100.0	3.5	3.2	6.5	68.9
Aged 30 to 34	44,638	2,088	1,881	2,601	30,845	100.0	4.7	4.2	5.8	69.1
Aged 35 to 44	100,530	4,886	2,563	6,173	67,555	100.0	4.9	2.5	6.1	67.2
Aged 45 to 54	109,113	6,038	4,095	3,624	80,279	100.0	5.5	3.8	3.3	73.6
Aged 55 to 64	67,956	2,920	1,490	2,003	52,282	100.0	4.3	2.2	2.9	76.9
Aged 65 to 74	26,117	1,620	135	424	19,351	100.0	6.2	0.5	1.6	74.1
Aged 75 to 84	13,985	724	493	229	10,343	100.0	5.2	3.5	1.6	74.0
Aged 85 or older	3,933	279	394	0	2,796	100.0	7.1	10.0	0.0	71.1
Arizona	**6,166,318**	**144,858**	**207,837**	**1,803,377**	**3,668,571**	**100.0**	**2.3**	**3.4**	**29.2**	**59.5**
Under age 18	1,626,855	32,130	62,232	675,313	730,217	100.0	2.0	3.8	41.5	44.9
Under age 5	479,145	10,370	16,308	216,304	200,818	100.0	2.2	3.4	45.1	41.9
Aged 5 to 9	444,018	8,315	16,790	187,743	196,766	100.0	1.9	3.8	42.3	44.3
Aged 10 to 14	436,903	8,042	18,667	174,872	201,229	100.0	1.8	4.3	40.0	46.1
Aged 15 to 17	266,789	5,403	10,467	96,394	131,404	100.0	2.0	3.9	36.1	49.3
Aged 18 to 19	165,970	3,899	6,044	58,703	81,606	100.0	2.3	3.6	35.4	49.2
Aged 20 to 24	420,118	9,376	16,524	147,242	220,206	100.0	2.2	3.9	35.0	52.4
Aged 25 to 29	469,834	14,598	17,493	174,553	237,383	100.0	3.1	3.7	37.2	50.5
Aged 30 to 34	429,697	16,368	16,945	160,861	214,919	100.0	3.8	3.9	37.4	50.0
Aged 35 to 44	857,846	28,254	31,495	250,344	503,972	100.0	3.3	3.7	29.2	58.7
Aged 45 to 54	787,098	17,519	26,690	164,576	542,380	100.0	2.2	3.4	20.9	68.9
Aged 55 to 64	619,149	12,246	16,481	90,482	477,249	100.0	2.0	2.7	14.6	77.1
Aged 65 to 74	405,034	6,856	8,546	47,806	326,616	100.0	1.7	2.1	11.8	80.6
Aged 75 to 84	292,120	2,915	3,969	26,500	251,698	100.0	1.0	1.4	9.1	86.2
Aged 85 or older	92,597	697	1,418	6,997	82,325	100.0	0.8	1.5	7.6	88.9

	total	Asian	black	Hispanic	non-Hispanic white	total	Asian	black	Hispanic	non-Hispanic white
Arkansas	**2,810,872**	**28,168**	**437,680**	**138,283**	**2,145,922**	**100.0%**	**1.0%**	**15.6%**	**4.9%**	**76.3%**
Under age 18	693,036	7,651	136,061	52,558	473,840	100.0	1.1	19.6	7.6	68.4
Under age 5	194,741	1,928	38,463	18,615	129,438	100.0	1.0	19.8	9.6	66.5
Aged 5 to 9	194,953	2,780	36,542	14,558	132,904	100.0	1.4	18.7	7.5	68.2
Aged 10 to 14	184,070	1,951	37,401	12,998	125,729	100.0	1.1	20.3	7.1	68.3
Aged 15 to 17	119,272	992	23,655	6,387	85,769	100.0	0.8	19.8	5.4	71.9
Aged 18 to 19	80,272	904	15,135	4,012	58,699	100.0	1.1	18.9	5.0	73.1
Aged 20 to 24	190,239	2,127	38,176	13,302	133,421	100.0	1.1	20.1	7.0	70.1
Aged 25 to 29	191,598	1,864	30,324	14,893	140,342	100.0	1.0	15.8	7.8	73.2
Aged 30 to 34	174,824	3,040	28,271	13,895	125,052	100.0	1.7	16.2	7.9	71.5
Aged 35 to 44	384,263	3,932	59,176	20,301	295,094	100.0	1.0	15.4	5.3	76.8
Aged 45 to 54	390,827	5,098	59,778	11,262	307,700	100.0	1.3	15.3	2.9	78.7
Aged 55 to 64	316,953	1,938	34,432	5,380	268,580	100.0	0.6	10.9	1.7	84.7
Aged 65 to 74	203,152	1,092	18,273	1,978	178,982	100.0	0.5	9.0	1.0	88.1
Aged 75 to 84	135,225	320	10,783	651	122,167	100.0	0.2	8.0	0.5	90.3
Aged 85 or older	50,483	202	7,271	51	42,045	100.0	0.4	14.4	0.1	83.3
California	**36,457,549**	**4,483,252**	**2,260,648**	**13,074,155**	**15,600,175**	**100.0**	**12.3**	**6.2**	**35.9**	**42.8**
Under age 18	9,531,046	950,214	640,147	4,598,703	2,954,713	100.0	10.0	6.7	48.2	31.0
Under age 5	2,672,666	257,728	162,948	1,384,142	754,798	100.0	9.6	6.1	51.8	28.2
Aged 5 to 9	2,514,639	245,864	166,414	1,249,117	750,500	100.0	9.8	6.6	49.7	29.8
Aged 10 to 14	2,700,465	274,347	188,616	1,257,439	874,102	100.0	10.2	7.0	46.6	32.4
Aged 15 to 17	1,643,276	172,275	122,169	708,005	575,313	100.0	10.5	7.4	43.1	35.0
Aged 18 to 19	1,095,451	122,796	80,652	446,122	398,710	100.0	11.2	7.4	40.7	36.4
Aged 20 to 24	2,697,878	315,259	174,253	1,128,042	993,863	100.0	11.7	6.5	41.8	36.8
Aged 25 to 29	2,629,253	320,755	148,735	1,165,257	911,850	100.0	12.2	5.7	44.3	34.7
Aged 30 to 34	2,603,007	384,458	152,292	1,113,940	887,934	100.0	14.8	5.9	42.8	34.1
Aged 35 to 44	5,525,036	770,694	356,328	1,955,045	2,315,882	100.0	13.9	6.4	35.4	41.9
Aged 45 to 54	5,017,599	672,491	314,648	1,313,579	2,604,336	100.0	13.4	6.3	26.2	51.9
Aged 55 to 64	3,430,449	450,162	194,212	701,219	2,011,964	100.0	13.1	5.7	20.4	58.7
Aged 65 to 74	2,002,937	275,350	114,530	370,561	1,206,165	100.0	13.7	5.7	18.5	60.2
Aged 75 to 84	1,400,449	167,110	62,830	224,401	929,079	100.0	11.9	4.5	16.0	66.3
Aged 85 or older	524,444	53,963	22,021	57,286	385,679	100.0	10.3	4.2	10.9	73.5
Colorado	**4,753,377**	**133,079**	**177,902**	**934,410**	**3,400,011**	**100.0**	**2.8**	**3.7**	**19.7**	**71.5**
Under age 18	1,169,643	31,049	50,057	324,406	722,177	100.0	2.7	4.3	27.7	61.7
Under age 5	338,995	9,559	13,757	104,950	198,153	100.0	2.8	4.1	31.0	58.5
Aged 5 to 9	322,980	9,294	14,049	92,991	194,715	100.0	2.9	4.3	28.8	60.3
Aged 10 to 14	313,386	8,657	13,678	81,380	198,702	100.0	2.8	4.4	26.0	63.4
Aged 15 to 17	194,282	3,539	8,573	45,085	130,607	100.0	1.8	4.4	23.2	67.2
Aged 18 to 19	127,504	2,975	5,739	27,516	86,248	100.0	2.3	4.5	21.6	67.6
Aged 20 to 24	337,730	11,107	14,023	76,751	225,409	100.0	3.3	4.2	22.7	66.7
Aged 25 to 29	365,092	11,614	13,424	92,383	239,960	100.0	3.2	3.7	25.3	65.7
Aged 30 to 34	346,409	14,916	13,349	88,745	222,794	100.0	4.3	3.9	25.6	64.3
Aged 35 to 44	720,020	24,217	29,505	134,207	521,978	100.0	3.4	4.1	18.6	72.5
Aged 45 to 54	720,742	18,222	26,594	92,266	570,776	100.0	2.5	3.7	12.8	79.2
Aged 55 to 64	489,352	9,890	13,863	51,414	406,513	100.0	2.0	2.8	10.5	83.1
Aged 65 to 74	256,742	5,286	7,079	28,341	212,660	100.0	2.1	2.8	11.0	82.8
Aged 75 to 84	161,816	2,944	2,682	15,166	139,429	100.0	1.8	1.7	9.4	86.2
Aged 85 or older	58,327	859	1,587	3,215	52,067	100.0	1.5	2.7	5.5	89.3

	total	Asian	black	Hispanic	non-Hispanic white	total	Asian	black	Hispanic	non-Hispanic white
Connecticut	**3,504,809**	**117,054**	**332,711**	**391,935**	**2,610,863**	**100.0%**	**3.3%**	**9.5%**	**11.2%**	**74.5%**
Under age 18	817,866	27,936	99,072	127,566	544,479	100.0	3.4	12.1	15.6	66.6
Under age 5	202,071	8,502	24,153	35,667	128,094	100.0	4.2	12.0	17.7	63.4
Aged 5 to 9	224,594	9,685	24,166	37,614	148,311	100.0	4.3	10.8	16.7	66.0
Aged 10 to 14	239,033	5,963	31,422	33,398	162,775	100.0	2.5	13.1	14.0	68.1
Aged 15 to 17	152,168	3,786	19,331	20,887	105,299	100.0	2.5	12.7	13.7	69.2
Aged 18 to 19	97,951	2,708	10,409	13,068	69,687	100.0	2.8	10.6	13.3	71.1
Aged 20 to 24	221,481	9,100	26,609	32,370	148,571	100.0	4.1	12.0	14.6	67.1
Aged 25 to 29	198,582	10,445	23,475	37,881	122,065	100.0	5.3	11.8	19.1	61.5
Aged 30 to 34	209,348	13,133	23,007	35,619	134,915	100.0	6.3	11.0	17.0	64.4
Aged 35 to 44	545,542	22,787	52,362	63,614	400,261	100.0	4.2	9.6	11.7	73.4
Aged 45 to 54	551,480	15,322	43,995	41,400	444,927	100.0	2.8	8.0	7.5	80.7
Aged 55 to 64	392,094	8,905	27,456	22,788	329,185	100.0	2.3	7.0	5.8	84.0
Aged 65 to 74	225,872	4,773	15,916	11,469	192,489	100.0	2.1	7.0	5.1	85.2
Aged 75 to 84	169,048	1,316	7,729	4,880	153,739	100.0	0.8	4.6	2.9	90.9
Aged 85 or older	75,545	629	2,681	1,280	70,545	100.0	0.8	3.5	1.7	93.4
Delaware	**853,476**	**24,413**	**176,845**	**53,836**	**586,778**	**100.0**	**2.9**	**20.7**	**6.3**	**68.8**
Under age 18	203,736	6,355	51,657	20,042	119,834	100.0	3.1	25.4	9.8	58.8
Under age 5	57,091	2,310	13,844	7,223	30,955	100.0	4.0	24.2	12.7	54.2
Aged 5 to 9	56,193	2,058	13,981	5,570	33,252	100.0	3.7	24.9	9.9	59.2
Aged 10 to 14	54,623	1,290	14,333	4,505	33,136	100.0	2.4	26.2	8.2	60.7
Aged 15 to 17	35,829	697	9,499	2,744	22,491	100.0	1.9	26.5	7.7	62.8
Aged 18 to 19	25,541	202	6,554	2,064	16,582	100.0	0.8	25.7	8.1	64.9
Aged 20 to 24	57,887	1,411	13,703	4,356	37,541	100.0	2.4	23.7	7.5	64.9
Aged 25 to 29	56,637	2,643	12,789	5,527	35,177	100.0	4.7	22.6	9.8	62.1
Aged 30 to 34	53,050	3,123	11,798	5,576	31,802	100.0	5.9	22.2	10.5	59.9
Aged 35 to 44	125,406	4,583	27,584	8,610	83,569	100.0	3.7	22.0	6.9	66.6
Aged 45 to 54	122,004	2,591	23,911	3,886	90,610	100.0	2.1	19.6	3.2	74.3
Aged 55 to 64	94,661	1,680	15,214	2,091	75,286	100.0	1.8	16.1	2.2	79.5
Aged 65 to 74	60,623	1,380	8,134	1,272	49,205	100.0	2.3	13.4	2.1	81.2
Aged 75 to 84	39,772	445	4,206	244	34,476	100.0	1.1	10.6	0.6	86.7
Aged 85 or older	14,159	0	1,295	168	12,696	100.0	0.0	9.1	1.2	89.7
District of Columbia	**581,530**	**19,827**	**322,105**	**47,775**	**183,519**	**100.0**	**3.4**	**55.4**	**8.2**	**31.6**
Under age 18	114,830	2,260	80,784	11,072	18,008	100.0	2.0	70.4	9.6	15.7
Under age 5	34,980	872	21,811	3,672	7,602	100.0	2.5	62.4	10.5	21.7
Aged 5 to 9	29,331	603	20,425	3,176	4,727	100.0	2.1	69.6	10.8	16.1
Aged 10 to 14	31,081	386	23,958	2,677	3,484	100.0	1.2	77.1	8.6	11.2
Aged 15 to 17	19,438	399	14,590	1,547	2,195	100.0	2.1	75.1	8.0	11.3
Aged 18 to 19	19,797	827	9,630	2,028	6,751	100.0	4.2	48.6	10.2	34.1
Aged 20 to 24	51,273	1,867	21,958	3,898	23,177	100.0	3.6	42.8	7.6	45.2
Aged 25 to 29	56,455	3,784	21,150	6,431	24,008	100.0	6.7	37.5	11.4	42.5
Aged 30 to 34	48,063	2,939	18,828	5,381	20,440	100.0	6.1	39.2	11.2	42.5
Aged 35 to 44	84,648	3,139	42,312	8,091	29,926	100.0	3.7	50.0	9.6	35.4
Aged 45 to 54	75,160	2,185	46,212	5,192	20,403	100.0	2.9	61.5	6.9	27.1
Aged 55 to 64	59,849	1,254	34,689	3,117	20,394	100.0	2.1	58.0	5.2	34.1
Aged 65 to 74	36,338	944	23,260	1,731	10,308	100.0	2.6	64.0	4.8	28.4
Aged 75 to 84	26,199	548	17,489	795	7,258	100.0	2.1	66.8	3.0	27.7
Aged 85 or older	8,918	80	5,793	39	2,846	100.0	0.9	65.0	0.4	31.9

	total	Asian	black	Hispanic	non-Hispanic white	total	Asian	black	Hispanic	non-Hispanic white
Florida	**18,089,889**	**393,427**	**2,778,549**	**3,642,989**	**11,040,168**	**100.0%**	**2.2%**	**15.4%**	**20.1%**	**61.0%**
Under age 18	4,018,644	86,945	852,284	957,137	2,017,601	100.0	2.2	21.2	23.8	50.2
Under age 5	1,117,630	24,761	240,906	299,598	516,674	100.0	2.2	21.6	26.8	46.2
Aged 5 to 9	1,055,789	26,302	214,495	249,221	541,544	100.0	2.5	20.3	23.6	51.3
Aged 10 to 14	1,127,349	21,189	242,818	257,658	574,509	100.0	1.9	21.5	22.9	51.0
Aged 15 to 17	717,876	14,693	154,065	150,660	384,874	100.0	2.0	21.5	21.0	53.6
Aged 18 to 19	456,718	12,122	99,761	103,838	232,786	100.0	2.7	21.8	22.7	51.0
Aged 20 to 24	1,154,089	24,779	235,548	274,698	605,823	100.0	2.1	20.4	23.8	52.5
Aged 25 to 29	1,147,634	26,479	212,815	292,278	602,873	100.0	2.3	18.5	25.5	52.5
Aged 30 to 34	1,099,501	38,202	183,318	300,793	563,684	100.0	3.5	16.7	27.4	51.3
Aged 35 to 44	2,602,876	73,572	406,145	611,059	1,486,998	100.0	2.8	15.6	23.5	57.1
Aged 45 to 54	2,534,472	59,503	356,615	446,009	1,644,811	100.0	2.3	14.1	17.6	64.9
Aged 55 to 64	2,041,838	40,414	213,551	288,595	1,479,865	100.0	2.0	10.5	14.1	72.5
Aged 65 to 74	1,452,008	19,915	128,252	200,747	1,096,977	100.0	1.4	8.8	13.8	75.5
Aged 75 to 84	1,171,721	9,122	69,524	126,634	963,787	100.0	0.8	5.9	10.8	82.3
Aged 85 or older	410,388	2,374	20,736	41,201	344,963	100.0	0.6	5.1	10.0	84.1
Georgia	**9,363,941**	**254,899**	**2,794,300**	**696,146**	**5,501,019**	**100.0**	**2.7**	**29.8**	**7.4**	**58.7**
Under age 18	2,452,225	60,523	844,373	247,379	1,247,843	100.0	2.5	34.4	10.1	50.9
Under age 5	698,935	16,900	224,302	98,184	341,555	100.0	2.4	32.1	14.0	48.9
Aged 5 to 9	671,546	16,540	230,558	70,607	338,465	100.0	2.5	34.3	10.5	50.4
Aged 10 to 14	668,385	16,751	239,442	51,066	348,198	100.0	2.5	35.8	7.6	52.1
Aged 15 to 17	413,359	10,332	150,071	27,522	219,625	100.0	2.5	36.3	6.7	53.1
Aged 18 to 19	291,744	7,828	100,131	19,889	157,686	100.0	2.7	34.3	6.8	54.0
Aged 20 to 24	651,722	15,104	217,085	63,094	347,374	100.0	2.3	33.3	9.7	53.3
Aged 25 to 29	665,568	21,715	207,301	83,843	346,625	100.0	3.3	31.1	12.6	52.1
Aged 30 to 34	673,099	29,587	205,606	80,965	349,814	100.0	4.4	30.5	12.0	52.0
Aged 35 to 44	1,472,645	49,699	439,918	115,107	855,207	100.0	3.4	29.9	7.8	58.1
Aged 45 to 54	1,316,787	35,734	376,904	51,009	839,934	100.0	2.7	28.6	3.9	63.8
Aged 55 to 64	933,272	20,581	218,562	21,124	666,269	100.0	2.2	23.4	2.3	71.4
Aged 65 to 74	505,861	9,028	108,725	9,107	376,528	100.0	1.8	21.5	1.8	74.4
Aged 75 to 84	294,712	4,185	54,199	3,735	231,264	100.0	1.4	18.4	1.3	78.5
Aged 85 or older	106,306	915	21,496	894	82,475	100.0	0.9	20.2	0.8	77.6
Hawaii	**1,285,498**	**512,995**	**28,062**	**99,664**	**315,822**	**100.0**	**39.9**	**2.2**	**7.8**	**24.6**
Under age 18	297,233	83,986	6,767	35,490	52,857	100.0	28.3	2.3	11.9	17.8
Under age 5	87,179	23,847	1,889	12,008	13,853	100.0	27.4	2.2	13.8	15.9
Aged 5 to 9	76,819	21,505	1,226	9,461	14,098	100.0	28.0	1.6	12.3	18.4
Aged 10 to 14	81,973	22,694	2,356	9,139	15,157	100.0	27.7	2.9	11.1	18.5
Aged 15 to 17	51,262	15,940	1,296	4,882	9,749	100.0	31.1	2.5	9.5	19.0
Aged 18 to 19	33,176	9,302	1,612	3,584	7,124	100.0	28.0	4.9	10.8	21.5
Aged 20 to 24	92,070	28,069	3,084	9,438	25,715	100.0	30.5	3.3	10.3	27.9
Aged 25 to 29	90,626	27,667	2,735	9,279	26,118	100.0	30.5	3.0	10.2	28.8
Aged 30 to 34	85,003	29,872	2,086	8,682	22,166	100.0	35.1	2.5	10.2	26.1
Aged 35 to 44	181,026	74,153	6,164	13,054	45,008	100.0	41.0	3.4	7.2	24.9
Aged 45 to 54	183,025	81,844	2,441	10,097	50,880	100.0	44.7	1.3	5.5	27.8
Aged 55 to 64	144,327	68,122	1,719	5,553	44,905	100.0	47.2	1.2	3.8	31.1
Aged 65 to 74	84,757	47,930	539	2,521	21,048	100.0	56.5	0.6	3.0	24.8
Aged 75 to 84	69,131	45,346	577	1,657	14,159	100.0	65.6	0.8	2.4	20.5
Aged 85 or older	25,124	16,704	338	309	5,842	100.0	66.5	1.3	1.2	23.3

	total	Asian	black	Hispanic	non-Hispanic white	total	Asian	black	Hispanic	non-Hispanic white
Idaho	**1,466,465**	**15,335**	**–**	**138,871**	**1,265,241**	**100.0%**	**1.0%**	**–**	**9.5%**	**86.3%**
Under age 18	394,315	3,196	–	54,652	319,318	100.0	0.8	–	13.9	81.0
Under age 5	112,366	1,213	–	16,031	90,449	100.0	1.1	–	14.3	80.5
Aged 5 to 9	107,521	648	–	16,894	85,590	100.0	0.6	–	15.7	79.6
Aged 10 to 14	106,092	912	–	13,315	86,207	100.0	0.9	–	12.6	81.3
Aged 15 to 17	68,336	423	–	8,412	57,072	100.0	0.6	–	12.3	83.5
Aged 18 to 19	44,994	787	–	5,500	36,927	100.0	1.7	–	12.2	82.1
Aged 20 to 24	107,953	853	–	12,046	91,365	100.0	0.8	–	11.2	84.6
Aged 25 to 29	105,878	1,082	–	11,490	88,607	100.0	1.0	–	10.9	83.7
Aged 30 to 34	94,026	1,506	–	13,167	76,182	100.0	1.6	–	14.0	81.0
Aged 35 to 44	192,227	2,810	–	18,267	166,311	100.0	1.5	–	9.5	86.5
Aged 45 to 54	204,603	2,419	–	13,691	183,377	100.0	1.2	–	6.7	89.6
Aged 55 to 64	153,078	1,930	–	5,319	142,161	100.0	1.3	–	3.5	92.9
Aged 65 to 74	89,464	421	–	3,136	83,583	100.0	0.5	–	3.5	93.4
Aged 75 to 84	56,280	140	–	1,437	54,265	100.0	0.2	–	2.6	96.4
Aged 85 or older	23,647	191	–	166	23,145	100.0	0.8	–	0.7	97.9
Illinois	**12,831,970**	**536,992**	**1,898,346**	**1,888,439**	**8,357,564**	**100.0**	**4.2**	**14.8**	**14.7**	**65.1**
Under age 18	3,216,387	117,096	580,840	657,714	1,791,135	100.0	3.6	18.1	20.4	55.7
Under age 5	889,338	34,307	150,302	210,450	467,761	100.0	3.9	16.9	23.7	52.6
Aged 5 to 9	874,663	33,624	152,480	187,208	481,662	100.0	3.8	17.4	21.4	55.1
Aged 10 to 14	898,758	30,530	173,348	168,940	510,548	100.0	3.4	19.3	18.8	56.8
Aged 15 to 17	553,628	18,635	104,710	91,116	331,164	100.0	3.4	18.9	16.5	59.8
Aged 18 to 19	384,216	16,486	68,333	61,367	231,631	100.0	4.3	17.8	16.0	60.3
Aged 20 to 24	905,237	38,500	142,831	163,428	548,890	100.0	4.3	15.8	18.1	60.6
Aged 25 to 29	897,843	47,054	136,125	196,767	510,034	100.0	5.2	15.2	21.9	56.8
Aged 30 to 34	873,973	57,667	121,931	184,505	502,423	100.0	6.6	14.0	21.1	57.5
Aged 35 to 44	1,877,625	95,328	265,717	280,745	1,221,176	100.0	5.1	14.2	15.0	65.0
Aged 45 to 54	1,846,038	72,833	249,879	176,569	1,331,290	100.0	3.9	13.5	9.6	72.1
Aged 55 to 64	1,298,278	50,863	163,448	95,466	979,978	100.0	3.9	12.6	7.4	75.5
Aged 65 to 74	770,024	26,490	97,085	44,383	596,808	100.0	3.4	12.6	5.8	77.5
Aged 75 to 84	539,564	11,291	54,279	22,141	449,299	100.0	2.1	10.1	4.1	83.3
Aged 85 or older	222,785	3,384	17,878	5,354	194,900	100.0	1.5	8.0	2.4	87.5
Indiana	**6,313,520**	**81,054**	**551,864**	**299,398**	**5,291,080**	**100.0**	**1.3**	**8.7**	**4.7**	**83.8**
Under age 18	1,579,597	18,921	174,866	106,867	1,237,978	100.0	1.2	11.1	6.8	78.4
Under age 5	433,580	5,266	48,891	35,868	328,956	100.0	1.2	11.3	8.3	75.9
Aged 5 to 9	428,767	6,921	46,687	31,570	332,747	100.0	1.6	10.9	7.4	77.6
Aged 10 to 14	440,378	3,395	49,831	25,633	352,652	100.0	0.8	11.3	5.8	80.1
Aged 15 to 17	276,872	3,339	29,457	13,796	223,623	100.0	1.2	10.6	5.0	80.8
Aged 18 to 19	183,425	3,391	18,729	9,980	148,340	100.0	1.8	10.2	5.4	80.9
Aged 20 to 24	439,744	9,656	40,718	28,970	353,683	100.0	2.2	9.3	6.6	80.4
Aged 25 to 29	434,777	7,141	41,145	32,248	348,722	100.0	1.6	9.5	7.4	80.2
Aged 30 to 34	400,770	6,299	39,801	27,617	322,286	100.0	1.6	9.9	6.9	80.4
Aged 35 to 44	896,489	14,104	76,291	43,186	753,275	100.0	1.6	8.5	4.8	84.0
Aged 45 to 54	926,792	10,979	71,158	28,220	807,367	100.0	1.2	7.7	3.0	87.1
Aged 55 to 64	670,934	7,105	44,295	13,150	600,709	100.0	1.1	6.6	2.0	89.5
Aged 65 to 74	397,244	2,133	24,778	4,821	362,571	100.0	0.5	6.2	1.2	91.3
Aged 75 to 84	275,549	1,052	15,396	3,327	254,363	100.0	0.4	5.6	1.2	92.3
Aged 85 or older	108,199	273	4,687	1,012	101,786	100.0	0.3	4.3	0.9	94.1

	total	Asian	black	Hispanic	non-Hispanic white	total	Asian	black	Hispanic	non-Hispanic white
Iowa	**2,982,085**	**45,647**	**67,297**	**112,987**	**2,714,414**	**100.0%**	**1.5%**	**2.3%**	**3.8%**	**91.0%**
Under age 18	714,520	11,252	23,426	44,730	612,150	100.0	1.6	3.3	6.3	85.7
Under age 5	191,127	3,082	5,842	13,087	161,035	100.0	1.6	3.1	6.8	84.3
Aged 5 to 9	192,953	3,684	7,512	13,569	160,824	100.0	1.9	3.9	7.0	83.3
Aged 10 to 14	200,655	2,210	6,577	11,211	175,881	100.0	1.1	3.3	5.6	87.7
Aged 15 to 17	129,785	2,276	3,495	6,863	114,410	100.0	1.8	2.7	5.3	88.2
Aged 18 to 19	93,887	1,399	2,506	5,556	83,081	100.0	1.5	2.7	5.9	88.5
Aged 20 to 24	221,652	5,229	5,931	9,798	197,417	100.0	2.4	2.7	4.4	89.1
Aged 25 to 29	179,340	4,312	4,730	10,387	158,187	100.0	2.4	2.6	5.8	88.2
Aged 30 to 34	173,492	5,297	6,021	11,218	149,660	100.0	3.1	3.5	6.5	86.3
Aged 35 to 44	401,183	8,362	9,320	15,379	363,891	100.0	2.1	2.3	3.8	90.7
Aged 45 to 54	441,849	4,874	6,730	9,329	417,092	100.0	1.1	1.5	2.1	94.4
Aged 55 to 64	320,789	2,525	4,342	3,600	308,525	100.0	0.8	1.4	1.1	96.2
Aged 65 to 74	205,409	1,365	2,590	1,635	198,728	100.0	0.7	1.3	0.8	96.7
Aged 75 to 84	161,333	969	1,429	936	157,806	100.0	0.6	0.9	0.6	97.8
Aged 85 or older	68,631	63	272	419	67,877	100.0	0.1	0.4	0.6	98.9
Kansas	**2,764,075**	**60,646**	**153,560**	**236,351**	**2,237,607**	**100.0**	**2.2**	**5.6**	**8.6**	**81.0**
Under age 18	694,667	14,055	44,854	88,423	515,408	100.0	2.0	6.5	12.7	74.2
Under age 5	194,702	4,349	11,296	28,351	139,048	100.0	2.2	5.8	14.6	71.4
Aged 5 to 9	189,279	4,119	11,777	25,602	139,136	100.0	2.2	6.2	13.5	73.5
Aged 10 to 14	189,718	3,974	12,290	22,834	143,389	100.0	2.1	6.5	12.0	75.6
Aged 15 to 17	120,968	1,613	9,491	11,636	93,835	100.0	1.3	7.8	9.6	77.6
Aged 18 to 19	85,492	2,028	6,089	8,976	64,675	100.0	2.4	7.1	10.5	75.7
Aged 20 to 24	212,731	5,138	14,155	21,490	164,622	100.0	2.4	6.7	10.1	77.4
Aged 25 to 29	179,361	5,651	11,051	22,104	136,738	100.0	3.2	6.2	12.3	76.2
Aged 30 to 34	164,645	7,044	8,468	21,519	124,375	100.0	4.3	5.1	13.1	75.5
Aged 35 to 44	385,320	12,665	23,146	36,910	303,688	100.0	3.3	6.0	9.6	78.8
Aged 45 to 54	401,047	5,709	22,046	18,975	346,532	100.0	1.4	5.5	4.7	86.4
Aged 55 to 64	285,148	5,430	12,774	10,193	252,044	100.0	1.9	4.5	3.6	88.4
Aged 65 to 74	170,065	1,700	5,956	4,039	156,083	100.0	1.0	3.5	2.4	91.8
Aged 75 to 84	128,393	994	3,534	2,917	119,140	100.0	0.8	2.8	2.3	92.8
Aged 85 or older	57,206	232	1,487	805	54,302	100.0	0.4	2.6	1.4	94.9
Kentucky	**4,206,074**	**38,835**	**310,146**	**83,015**	**3,715,900**	**100.0**	**0.9**	**7.4**	**2.0**	**88.3**
Under age 18	1,000,341	8,594	89,516	27,004	847,109	100.0	0.9	8.9	2.7	84.7
Under age 5	276,964	3,075	25,094	9,791	230,599	100.0	1.1	9.1	3.5	83.3
Aged 5 to 9	269,020	2,238	23,261	7,525	226,752	100.0	0.8	8.6	2.8	84.3
Aged 10 to 14	278,788	1,926	23,820	6,252	239,244	100.0	0.7	8.5	2.2	85.8
Aged 15 to 17	175,569	1,355	17,341	3,436	150,514	100.0	0.8	9.9	2.0	85.7
Aged 18 to 19	116,037	583	11,322	3,053	98,660	100.0	0.5	9.8	2.6	85.0
Aged 20 to 24	276,924	3,519	26,742	8,202	234,723	100.0	1.3	9.7	3.0	84.8
Aged 25 to 29	302,031	3,752	21,163	8,834	264,524	100.0	1.2	7.0	2.9	87.6
Aged 30 to 34	270,797	5,020	20,325	9,254	232,908	100.0	1.9	7.5	3.4	86.0
Aged 35 to 44	612,669	8,445	45,453	15,133	539,616	100.0	1.4	7.4	2.5	88.1
Aged 45 to 54	618,932	4,051	44,089	6,117	559,127	100.0	0.7	7.1	1.0	90.3
Aged 55 to 64	473,040	2,960	25,730	3,078	437,357	100.0	0.6	5.4	0.7	92.5
Aged 65 to 74	285,566	1,239	14,691	1,628	266,582	100.0	0.4	5.1	0.6	93.4
Aged 75 to 84	183,197	554	7,644	549	172,875	100.0	0.3	4.2	0.3	94.4
Aged 85 or older	66,540	118	3,471	163	62,419	100.0	0.2	5.2	0.2	93.8

	total	Asian	black	Hispanic	non-Hispanic white	total	Asian	black	Hispanic	non-Hispanic white
Louisiana	**4,287,768**	**57,084**	**1,356,981**	**123,281**	**2,689,206**	**100.0%**	**1.3%**	**31.6%**	**2.9%**	**62.7%**
Under age 18	1,088,997	12,865	420,903	30,957	600,810	100.0	1.2	38.7	2.8	55.2
Under age 5	301,198	3,173	116,961	10,270	163,288	100.0	1.1	38.8	3.4	54.2
Aged 5 to 9	294,827	2,968	109,961	7,447	167,635	100.0	1.0	37.3	2.5	56.9
Aged 10 to 14	305,073	4,461	122,603	9,079	162,934	100.0	1.5	40.2	3.0	53.4
Aged 15 to 17	187,899	2,263	71,378	4,161	106,953	100.0	1.2	38.0	2.2	56.9
Aged 18 to 19	144,247	2,442	58,595	5,112	76,175	100.0	1.7	40.6	3.5	52.8
Aged 20 to 24	320,006	4,367	112,171	11,676	187,184	100.0	1.4	35.1	3.6	58.5
Aged 25 to 29	299,768	6,363	95,132	11,178	181,604	100.0	2.1	31.7	3.7	60.6
Aged 30 to 34	254,532	5,477	82,722	11,857	152,799	100.0	2.2	32.5	4.7	60.0
Aged 35 to 44	584,189	8,636	178,088	17,596	374,597	100.0	1.5	30.5	3.0	64.1
Aged 45 to 54	616,359	7,026	176,862	13,977	409,798	100.0	1.1	28.7	2.3	66.5
Aged 55 to 64	456,796	5,782	117,233	9,903	318,265	100.0	1.3	25.7	2.2	69.7
Aged 65 to 74	278,591	2,395	67,189	6,783	199,957	100.0	0.9	24.1	2.4	71.8
Aged 75 to 84	181,851	1,612	35,683	3,158	139,523	100.0	0.9	19.6	1.7	76.7
Aged 85 or older	62,432	119	12,403	1,084	48,494	100.0	0.2	19.9	1.7	77.7
Maine	**1,321,574**	**12,004**	**13,669**	**12,622**	**1,259,089**	**100.0**	**0.9**	**1.0**	**1.0**	**95.3**
Under age 18	281,872	3,640	6,119	4,304	259,976	100.0	1.3	2.2	1.5	92.2
Under age 5	70,227	1,386	1,679	1,469	64,418	100.0	2.0	2.4	2.1	91.7
Aged 5 to 9	72,033	702	1,587	1,461	65,940	100.0	1.0	2.2	2.0	91.5
Aged 10 to 14	83,029	662	1,702	846	77,450	100.0	0.8	2.0	1.0	93.3
Aged 15 to 17	56,583	890	1,151	528	52,168	100.0	1.6	2.0	0.9	92.2
Aged 18 to 19	34,386	371	935	594	31,476	100.0	1.1	2.7	1.7	91.5
Aged 20 to 24	81,988	528	1,330	1,550	76,491	100.0	0.6	1.6	1.9	93.3
Aged 25 to 29	75,710	1,070	641	1,075	71,291	100.0	1.4	0.8	1.4	94.2
Aged 30 to 34	76,282	1,623	954	1,112	70,626	100.0	2.1	1.3	1.5	92.6
Aged 35 to 44	194,089	1,562	1,828	1,224	185,864	100.0	0.8	0.9	0.6	95.8
Aged 45 to 54	217,754	1,718	971	1,308	210,913	100.0	0.8	0.4	0.6	96.9
Aged 55 to 64	167,059	740	745	857	163,276	100.0	0.4	0.4	0.5	97.7
Aged 65 to 74	98,317	440	99	457	96,157	100.0	0.4	0.1	0.5	97.8
Aged 75 to 84	68,040	243	47	141	67,143	100.0	0.4	0.1	0.2	98.7
Aged 85 or older	26,077	69	0	0	25,876	100.0	0.3	0.0	0.0	99.2
Maryland	**5,615,727**	**276,362**	**1,624,858**	**336,390**	**3,275,198**	**100.0**	**4.9**	**28.9**	**6.0**	**58.3**
Under age 18	1,362,132	60,550	446,219	105,681	701,424	100.0	4.4	32.8	7.8	51.5
Under age 5	368,501	17,848	119,421	35,328	179,043	100.0	4.8	32.4	9.6	48.6
Aged 5 to 9	363,536	17,506	117,110	28,468	185,780	100.0	4.8	32.2	7.8	51.1
Aged 10 to 14	382,153	15,408	126,476	26,657	202,645	100.0	4.0	33.1	7.0	53.0
Aged 15 to 17	247,942	9,788	83,212	15,228	133,956	100.0	3.9	33.6	6.1	54.0
Aged 18 to 19	164,785	7,497	54,248	9,680	90,347	100.0	4.5	32.9	5.9	54.8
Aged 20 to 24	371,298	16,883	118,396	29,062	199,307	100.0	4.5	31.9	7.8	53.7
Aged 25 to 29	363,534	20,744	113,834	35,160	188,607	100.0	5.7	31.3	9.7	51.9
Aged 30 to 34	354,344	26,794	106,025	33,413	181,751	100.0	7.6	29.9	9.4	51.3
Aged 35 to 44	880,892	52,626	266,697	58,357	492,578	100.0	6.0	30.3	6.6	55.9
Aged 45 to 54	860,739	40,821	235,941	34,888	538,328	100.0	4.7	27.4	4.1	62.5
Aged 55 to 64	610,671	27,445	150,943	16,925	409,167	100.0	4.5	24.7	2.8	67.0
Aged 65 to 74	341,696	15,162	79,574	7,472	236,431	100.0	4.4	23.3	2.2	69.2
Aged 75 to 84	223,325	5,756	38,329	4,963	172,979	100.0	2.6	17.2	2.2	77.5
Aged 85 or older	82,311	2,084	14,652	789	64,279	100.0	2.5	17.8	1.0	78.1

	total	Asian	black	Hispanic	non-Hispanic white	total	Asian	black	Hispanic	non-Hispanic white
Massachusetts	6,437,193	310,441	393,207	510,482	5,104,271	100.0%	4.8%	6.1%	7.9%	79.3%
Under age 18	1,448,477	70,021	116,144	167,128	1,050,950	100.0	4.8	8.0	11.5	72.6
Under age 5	387,619	21,201	33,032	46,181	269,851	100.0	5.5	8.5	11.9	69.6
Aged 5 to 9	386,105	22,144	28,052	45,705	278,889	100.0	5.7	7.3	11.8	72.2
Aged 10 to 14	413,693	16,315	33,782	46,446	306,083	100.0	3.9	8.2	11.2	74.0
Aged 15 to 17	261,060	10,361	21,278	28,796	196,127	100.0	4.0	8.2	11.0	75.1
Aged 18 to 19	189,182	11,256	15,897	18,970	138,771	100.0	5.9	8.4	10.0	73.4
Aged 20 to 24	453,973	26,793	34,866	50,223	329,178	100.0	5.9	7.7	11.1	72.5
Aged 25 to 29	403,690	29,758	27,763	47,826	288,851	100.0	7.4	6.9	11.8	71.6
Aged 30 to 34	413,360	36,978	26,671	46,295	296,032	100.0	8.9	6.5	11.2	71.6
Aged 35 to 44	992,955	57,615	63,909	79,479	778,742	100.0	5.8	6.4	8.0	78.4
Aged 45 to 54	972,639	36,653	50,462	51,948	821,290	100.0	3.8	5.2	5.3	84.4
Aged 55 to 64	706,031	21,619	29,404	27,698	619,672	100.0	3.1	4.2	3.9	87.8
Aged 65 to 74	412,051	12,261	16,378	14,641	365,216	100.0	3.0	4.0	3.6	88.6
Aged 75 to 84	309,373	6,369	9,188	4,602	286,199	100.0	2.1	3.0	1.5	92.5
Aged 85 or older	135,462	1,118	2,525	1,672	129,370	100.0	0.8	1.9	1.2	95.5
Michigan	10,095,643	236,972	1,426,809	392,770	7,836,885	100.0	2.3	14.1	3.9	77.6
Under age 18	2,477,421	57,781	433,495	138,227	1,763,173	100.0	2.3	17.5	5.6	71.2
Under age 5	639,239	16,465	105,405	40,094	450,841	100.0	2.6	16.5	6.3	70.5
Aged 5 to 9	657,808	17,318	112,824	40,803	462,550	100.0	2.6	17.2	6.2	70.3
Aged 10 to 14	721,956	14,742	130,423	37,060	518,673	100.0	2.0	18.1	5.1	71.8
Aged 15 to 17	458,418	9,256	84,843	20,270	331,109	100.0	2.0	18.5	4.4	72.2
Aged 18 to 19	293,094	6,920	46,238	15,084	217,312	100.0	2.4	15.8	5.1	74.1
Aged 20 to 24	686,462	17,398	100,330	32,720	520,640	100.0	2.5	14.6	4.8	75.8
Aged 25 to 29	638,447	21,464	102,231	35,715	467,170	100.0	3.4	16.0	5.6	73.2
Aged 30 to 34	623,116	28,341	98,638	35,750	446,874	100.0	4.5	15.8	5.7	71.7
Aged 35 to 44	1,469,671	45,198	203,517	59,000	1,138,646	100.0	3.1	13.8	4.0	77.5
Aged 45 to 54	1,536,628	27,995	191,948	39,074	1,255,550	100.0	1.8	12.5	2.5	81.7
Aged 55 to 64	1,110,437	17,980	127,915	21,687	929,839	100.0	1.6	11.5	2.0	83.7
Aged 65 to 74	640,733	8,597	66,324	9,544	549,388	100.0	1.3	10.4	1.5	85.7
Aged 75 to 84	446,703	4,404	40,863	4,994	393,060	100.0	1.0	9.1	1.1	88.0
Aged 85 or older	172,931	894	15,310	975	155,233	100.0	0.5	8.9	0.6	89.8
Minnesota	5,167,101	179,295	228,354	195,138	4,435,973	100.0	3.5	4.4	3.8	85.9
Under age 18	1,257,930	56,624	82,332	73,094	987,058	100.0	4.5	6.5	5.8	78.5
Under age 5	347,404	15,587	27,238	26,825	260,131	100.0	4.5	7.8	7.7	74.9
Aged 5 to 9	335,072	16,204	21,159	20,126	260,866	100.0	4.8	6.3	6.0	77.9
Aged 10 to 14	350,245	15,234	20,659	17,500	280,927	100.0	4.3	5.9	5.0	80.2
Aged 15 to 17	225,209	9,599	13,276	8,643	185,134	100.0	4.3	5.9	3.8	82.2
Aged 18 to 19	150,314	5,969	9,740	6,568	123,473	100.0	4.0	6.5	4.4	82.1
Aged 20 to 24	371,409	13,512	18,231	17,714	311,210	100.0	3.6	4.9	4.8	83.8
Aged 25 to 29	342,899	16,012	19,862	21,185	277,843	100.0	4.7	5.8	6.2	81.0
Aged 30 to 34	326,607	20,683	19,108	20,314	258,190	100.0	6.3	5.9	6.2	79.1
Aged 35 to 44	759,760	29,839	35,573	28,598	652,316	100.0	3.9	4.7	3.8	85.9
Aged 45 to 54	795,187	18,510	25,398	15,931	722,435	100.0	2.3	3.2	2.0	90.9
Aged 55 to 64	534,890	9,980	10,283	6,467	501,653	100.0	1.9	1.9	1.2	93.8
Aged 65 to 74	311,051	4,913	4,902	3,795	294,227	100.0	1.6	1.6	1.2	94.6
Aged 75 to 84	220,590	2,207	2,345	1,243	213,417	100.0	1.0	1.1	0.6	96.7
Aged 85 or older	96,464	1,046	580	229	94,151	100.0	1.1	0.6	0.2	97.6

	total	Asian	black	Hispanic	non-Hispanic white	total	Asian	black	Hispanic	non-Hispanic white
Mississippi	**2,910,540**	**22,116**	**1,087,114**	**46,348**	**1,724,848**	**100.0%**	**0.8%**	**37.4%**	**1.6%**	**59.3%**
Under age 18	758,927	4,483	341,684	13,942	386,127	100.0	0.6	45.0	1.8	50.9
Under age 5	206,089	1,045	90,923	5,538	104,726	100.0	0.5	44.1	2.7	50.8
Aged 5 to 9	197,451	1,008	87,203	2,750	102,322	100.0	0.5	44.2	1.4	51.8
Aged 10 to 14	222,284	1,589	104,015	3,570	110,535	100.0	0.7	46.8	1.6	49.7
Aged 15 to 17	133,103	841	59,543	2,084	68,544	100.0	0.6	44.7	1.6	51.5
Aged 18 to 19	96,932	427	42,788	1,832	50,916	100.0	0.4	44.1	1.9	52.5
Aged 20 to 24	214,999	2,624	93,188	6,263	109,774	100.0	1.2	43.3	2.9	51.1
Aged 25 to 29	195,506	2,029	78,269	6,675	107,155	100.0	1.0	40.0	3.4	54.8
Aged 30 to 34	171,768	2,290	64,737	4,316	99,771	100.0	1.3	37.7	2.5	58.1
Aged 35 to 44	398,694	4,251	146,823	4,907	240,024	100.0	1.1	36.8	1.2	60.2
Aged 45 to 54	405,857	2,371	143,360	4,948	251,229	100.0	0.6	35.3	1.2	61.9
Aged 55 to 64	307,164	1,546	89,003	1,752	212,557	100.0	0.5	29.0	0.6	69.2
Aged 65 to 74	192,151	1,239	48,951	1,165	139,553	100.0	0.6	25.5	0.6	72.6
Aged 75 to 84	120,948	666	25,681	233	93,628	100.0	0.6	21.2	0.2	77.4
Aged 85 or older	47,594	190	12,630	315	34,114	100.0	0.4	26.5	0.7	71.7
Missouri	**5,842,713**	**86,010**	**661,535**	**160,898**	**4,820,772**	**100.0**	**1.5**	**11.3**	**2.8**	**82.5**
Under age 18	1,422,429	21,746	202,465	57,964	1,091,479	100.0	1.5	14.2	4.1	76.7
Under age 5	390,715	6,407	54,353	22,015	292,014	100.0	1.6	13.9	5.6	74.7
Aged 5 to 9	383,940	6,096	53,565	16,406	293,301	100.0	1.6	14.0	4.3	76.4
Aged 10 to 14	393,812	6,042	57,339	12,216	305,807	100.0	1.5	14.6	3.1	77.7
Aged 15 to 17	253,962	3,201	37,208	7,327	200,357	100.0	1.3	14.7	2.9	78.9
Aged 18 to 19	165,621	2,209	21,778	6,893	131,103	100.0	1.3	13.1	4.2	79.2
Aged 20 to 24	405,388	7,308	50,749	14,475	325,522	100.0	1.8	12.5	3.6	80.3
Aged 25 to 29	400,567	8,000	49,051	15,389	321,915	100.0	2.0	12.2	3.8	80.4
Aged 30 to 34	357,364	9,953	44,372	14,086	282,192	100.0	2.8	12.4	3.9	79.0
Aged 35 to 44	815,052	13,685	91,708	21,712	675,139	100.0	1.7	11.3	2.7	82.8
Aged 45 to 54	863,408	11,301	90,927	14,985	732,525	100.0	1.3	10.5	1.7	84.8
Aged 55 to 64	633,279	7,321	52,963	7,752	557,997	100.0	1.2	8.4	1.2	88.1
Aged 65 to 74	395,919	2,809	32,250	3,926	352,686	100.0	0.7	8.1	1.0	89.1
Aged 75 to 84	275,684	1,542	18,579	3,101	250,187	100.0	0.6	6.7	1.1	90.8
Aged 85 or older	108,002	136	6,693	615	100,027	100.0	0.1	6.2	0.6	92.6
Montana	**944,632**	**5,525**	**–**	**20,513**	**836,541**	**100.0**	**0.6**	**–**	**2.2**	**88.6**
Under age 18	218,098	1,930	–	7,486	179,719	100.0	0.9	–	3.4	82.4
Under age 5	57,577	630	–	2,280	46,503	100.0	1.1	–	4.0	80.8
Aged 5 to 9	58,636	438	–	1,588	48,943	100.0	0.7	–	2.7	83.5
Aged 10 to 14	59,383	471	–	1,708	49,415	100.0	0.8	–	2.9	83.2
Aged 15 to 17	42,502	391	–	1,910	34,858	100.0	0.9	–	4.5	82.0
Aged 18 to 19	28,161	135	–	616	22,587	100.0	0.5	–	2.2	80.2
Aged 20 to 24	67,693	505	–	2,592	57,646	100.0	0.7	–	3.8	85.2
Aged 25 to 29	61,586	464	–	1,618	52,503	100.0	0.8	–	2.6	85.3
Aged 30 to 34	50,030	291	–	1,575	44,097	100.0	0.6	–	3.1	88.1
Aged 35 to 44	120,418	987	–	2,045	107,464	100.0	0.8	–	1.7	89.2
Aged 45 to 54	152,481	864	–	2,069	140,225	100.0	0.6	–	1.4	92.0
Aged 55 to 64	114,847	174	–	1,277	107,924	100.0	0.2	–	1.1	94.0
Aged 65 to 74	67,916	127	–	704	62,830	100.0	0.2	–	1.0	92.5
Aged 75 to 84	46,601	48	–	455	45,208	100.0	0.1	–	1.0	97.0
Aged 85 or older	16,801	0	–	76	16,338	100.0	0.0	–	0.5	97.2

	total	Asian	black	Hispanic	non-Hispanic white	total	Asian	black	Hispanic	non-Hispanic white
Nebraska	**1,768,331**	**29,815**	**72,095**	**130,230**	**1,500,166**	**100.0%**	**1.7%**	**4.1%**	**7.4%**	**84.8%**
Under age 18	445,410	7,057	24,040	51,463	346,153	100.0	1.6	5.4	11.6	77.7
Under age 5	128,307	1,947	7,352	17,712	95,527	100.0	1.5	5.7	13.8	74.5
Aged 5 to 9	120,167	2,044	6,499	16,019	91,136	100.0	1.7	5.4	13.3	75.8
Aged 10 to 14	119,132	1,664	6,306	11,260	95,848	100.0	1.4	5.3	9.5	80.5
Aged 15 to 17	77,804	1,402	3,883	6,472	63,642	100.0	1.8	5.0	8.3	81.8
Aged 18 to 19	55,028	1,304	1,925	5,606	44,584	100.0	2.4	3.5	10.2	81.0
Aged 20 to 24	132,025	2,717	5,804	9,600	111,129	100.0	2.1	4.4	7.3	84.2
Aged 25 to 29	117,732	2,934	5,785	12,167	93,334	100.0	2.5	4.9	10.3	79.3
Aged 30 to 34	112,177	4,140	4,973	14,812	86,185	100.0	3.7	4.4	13.2	76.8
Aged 35 to 44	233,713	3,862	10,385	16,880	199,280	100.0	1.7	4.4	7.2	85.3
Aged 45 to 54	256,350	3,407	8,966	11,041	229,793	100.0	1.3	3.5	4.3	89.6
Aged 55 to 64	182,621	2,978	5,514	5,509	167,050	100.0	1.6	3.0	3.0	91.5
Aged 65 to 74	112,624	850	3,513	2,094	105,510	100.0	0.8	3.1	1.9	93.7
Aged 75 to 84	84,072	551	885	829	81,299	100.0	0.7	1.1	1.0	96.7
Aged 85 or older	36,579	15	305	229	35,849	100.0	0.0	0.8	0.6	98.0
Nevada	**2,495,529**	**147,363**	**183,064**	**610,051**	**1,463,452**	**100.0**	**5.9**	**7.3**	**24.4**	**58.6**
Under age 18	634,447	30,471	54,965	222,751	290,741	100.0	4.8	8.7	35.1	45.8
Under age 5	183,437	9,302	16,214	69,588	77,174	100.0	5.1	8.8	37.9	42.1
Aged 5 to 9	169,201	7,014	14,889	62,396	74,977	100.0	4.1	8.8	36.9	44.3
Aged 10 to 14	177,454	8,871	14,432	59,373	85,244	100.0	5.0	8.1	33.5	48.0
Aged 15 to 17	104,355	5,284	9,430	31,394	53,346	100.0	5.1	9.0	30.1	51.1
Aged 18 to 19	58,962	2,514	4,762	16,096	31,986	100.0	4.3	8.1	27.3	54.2
Aged 20 to 24	157,800	7,443	13,448	47,575	81,206	100.0	4.7	8.5	30.1	51.5
Aged 25 to 29	192,667	12,441	13,866	61,578	98,029	100.0	6.5	7.2	32.0	50.9
Aged 30 to 34	179,676	12,129	13,439	59,826	88,243	100.0	6.8	7.5	33.3	49.1
Aged 35 to 44	382,576	26,049	28,261	98,445	219,805	100.0	6.8	7.4	25.7	57.5
Aged 45 to 54	340,076	23,555	23,383	52,754	231,054	100.0	6.9	6.9	15.5	67.9
Aged 55 to 64	274,299	17,469	16,079	28,776	205,193	100.0	6.4	5.9	10.5	74.8
Aged 65 to 74	156,780	10,017	9,726	13,817	120,115	100.0	6.4	6.2	8.8	76.6
Aged 75 to 84	92,570	4,423	4,290	7,124	74,840	100.0	4.8	4.6	7.7	80.8
Aged 85 or older	25,676	852	845	1,309	22,240	100.0	3.3	3.3	5.1	86.6
New Hampshire	**1,314,895**	**26,136**	**13,842**	**29,721**	**1,230,377**	**100.0**	**2.0**	**1.1**	**2.3**	**93.6**
Under age 18	297,678	7,020	3,933	9,836	271,231	100.0	2.4	1.3	3.3	91.1
Under age 5	73,480	2,173	1,177	3,088	65,684	100.0	3.0	1.6	4.2	89.4
Aged 5 to 9	78,862	1,688	807	2,556	71,488	100.0	2.1	1.0	3.2	90.6
Aged 10 to 14	87,274	2,386	1,254	2,735	79,784	100.0	2.7	1.4	3.1	91.4
Aged 15 to 17	58,062	773	695	1,457	54,275	100.0	1.3	1.2	2.5	93.5
Aged 18 to 19	37,952	837	390	1,538	34,346	100.0	2.2	1.0	4.1	90.5
Aged 20 to 24	82,393	1,198	2,284	1,773	76,653	100.0	1.5	2.8	2.2	93.0
Aged 25 to 29	75,753	1,640	1,280	2,780	69,203	100.0	2.2	1.7	3.7	91.4
Aged 30 to 34	78,212	3,987	600	3,201	69,684	100.0	5.1	0.8	4.1	89.1
Aged 35 to 44	208,140	5,183	2,818	4,793	193,489	100.0	2.5	1.4	2.3	93.0
Aged 45 to 54	217,645	3,285	1,011	3,009	208,622	100.0	1.5	0.5	1.4	95.9
Aged 55 to 64	155,286	1,641	1,327	1,755	148,957	100.0	1.1	0.9	1.1	95.9
Aged 65 to 74	83,356	949	199	919	80,386	100.0	1.1	0.2	1.1	96.4
Aged 75 to 84	55,432	396	0	117	54,758	100.0	0.7	0.0	0.2	98.8
Aged 85 or older	23,048	0	0	0	23,048	100.0	0.0	0.0	0.0	100.0

	total	Asian	black	Hispanic	non-Hispanic white	total	Asian	black	Hispanic	non-Hispanic white
New Jersey	**8,724,560**	**652,378**	**1,187,161**	**1,364,699**	**5,431,103**	**100.0%**	**7.5%**	**13.6%**	**15.6%**	**62.3%**
Under age 18	2,089,653	154,131	334,782	397,242	1,164,692	100.0	7.4	16.0	19.0	55.7
Under age 5	559,872	43,695	87,113	126,231	288,515	100.0	7.8	15.6	22.5	51.5
Aged 5 to 9	565,814	46,385	83,719	104,662	320,510	100.0	8.2	14.8	18.5	56.6
Aged 10 to 14	592,696	39,950	102,030	105,462	335,942	100.0	6.7	17.2	17.8	56.7
Aged 15 to 17	371,271	24,101	61,920	60,887	219,725	100.0	6.5	16.7	16.4	59.2
Aged 18 to 19	226,345	13,568	40,120	38,982	131,337	100.0	6.0	17.7	17.2	58.0
Aged 20 to 24	537,322	33,956	87,720	110,073	299,194	100.0	6.3	16.3	20.5	55.7
Aged 25 to 29	511,804	48,154	81,134	125,101	249,479	100.0	9.4	15.9	24.4	48.7
Aged 30 to 34	570,969	69,080	81,417	124,794	290,007	100.0	12.1	14.3	21.9	50.8
Aged 35 to 44	1,393,015	130,749	190,774	232,413	826,713	100.0	9.4	13.7	16.7	59.3
Aged 45 to 54	1,325,391	96,335	159,376	158,553	904,864	100.0	7.3	12.0	12.0	68.3
Aged 55 to 64	944,456	60,762	104,335	94,549	680,622	100.0	6.4	11.0	10.0	72.1
Aged 65 to 74	559,820	29,495	63,652	52,013	411,231	100.0	5.3	11.4	9.3	73.5
Aged 75 to 84	402,259	13,499	32,189	24,407	330,812	100.0	3.4	8.0	6.1	82.2
Aged 85 or older	163,526	2,649	11,662	6,572	142,152	100.0	1.6	7.1	4.0	86.9
New Mexico	**1,954,599**	**25,983**	**39,654**	**860,687**	**828,965**	**100.0**	**1.3**	**2.0**	**44.0**	**42.4**
Under age 18	510,350	5,557	12,954	269,427	155,326	100.0	1.1	2.5	52.8	30.4
Under age 5	141,732	1,846	2,487	77,735	41,517	100.0	1.3	1.8	54.8	29.3
Aged 5 to 9	135,446	1,524	4,097	73,868	39,043	100.0	1.1	3.0	54.5	28.8
Aged 10 to 14	144,396	1,315	4,108	72,831	47,006	100.0	0.9	2.8	50.4	32.6
Aged 15 to 17	88,776	872	2,262	44,993	27,760	100.0	1.0	2.5	50.7	31.3
Aged 18 to 19	58,823	721	1,467	31,035	17,630	100.0	1.2	2.5	52.8	30.0
Aged 20 to 24	145,993	1,418	3,872	71,908	50,950	100.0	1.0	2.7	49.3	34.9
Aged 25 to 29	133,813	2,871	2,700	65,133	47,767	100.0	2.1	2.0	48.7	35.7
Aged 30 to 34	123,019	2,718	3,085	62,183	43,336	100.0	2.2	2.5	50.5	35.2
Aged 35 to 44	260,001	4,292	5,560	115,017	108,161	100.0	1.7	2.1	44.2	41.6
Aged 45 to 54	270,937	3,360	4,349	102,690	137,076	100.0	1.2	1.6	37.9	50.6
Aged 55 to 64	210,384	3,209	3,162	67,738	121,522	100.0	1.5	1.5	32.2	57.8
Aged 65 to 74	127,571	1,159	1,029	42,362	75,474	100.0	0.9	0.8	33.2	59.2
Aged 75 to 84	85,009	579	738	25,454	53,885	100.0	0.7	0.9	29.9	63.4
Aged 85 or older	28,699	99	738	7,740	17,838	100.0	0.3	2.6	27.0	62.2
New York	**19,306,183**	**1,322,971**	**2,990,260**	**3,139,590**	**11,628,557**	**100.0**	**6.9**	**15.5**	**16.3**	**60.2**
Under age 18	4,513,489	279,750	834,501	913,346	2,403,698	100.0	6.2	18.5	20.2	53.3
Under age 5	1,221,010	82,878	219,626	267,862	620,397	100.0	6.8	18.0	21.9	50.8
Aged 5 to 9	1,196,762	78,001	220,693	240,829	634,056	100.0	6.5	18.4	20.1	53.0
Aged 10 to 14	1,281,783	73,075	235,169	253,683	698,199	100.0	5.7	18.3	19.8	54.5
Aged 15 to 17	813,934	45,796	159,013	150,972	451,046	100.0	5.6	19.5	18.5	55.4
Aged 18 to 19	580,825	35,477	99,177	102,457	335,340	100.0	6.1	17.1	17.6	57.7
Aged 20 to 24	1,365,987	97,648	238,646	263,567	748,643	100.0	7.1	17.5	19.3	54.8
Aged 25 to 29	1,253,355	110,862	207,621	275,457	644,894	100.0	8.8	16.6	22.0	51.5
Aged 30 to 34	1,255,764	128,512	191,462	258,550	663,000	100.0	10.2	15.2	20.6	52.8
Aged 35 to 44	2,903,901	236,192	450,295	497,419	1,687,580	100.0	8.1	15.5	17.1	58.1
Aged 45 to 54	2,823,776	197,342	404,513	369,534	1,826,401	100.0	7.0	14.3	13.1	64.7
Aged 55 to 64	2,088,198	126,237	273,893	238,920	1,431,706	100.0	6.0	13.1	11.4	68.6
Aged 65 to 74	1,268,161	70,459	167,792	132,272	889,989	100.0	5.6	13.2	10.4	70.2
Aged 75 to 84	894,543	29,487	90,218	66,834	704,895	100.0	3.3	10.1	7.5	78.8
Aged 85 or older	358,184	11,005	32,142	21,234	292,411	100.0	3.1	9.0	5.9	81.6

	total	Asian	black	Hispanic	non-Hispanic white	total	Asian	black	Hispanic	non-Hispanic white
North Carolina	**8,856,505**	**162,578**	**1,892,469**	**597,382**	**5,999,236**	**100.0%**	**1.8%**	**21.4%**	**6.7%**	**67.7%**
Under age 18	2,155,019	42,426	535,708	214,793	1,280,257	100.0	2.0	24.9	10.0	59.4
Under age 5	602,733	11,107	134,839	83,871	345,904	100.0	1.8	22.4	13.9	57.4
Aged 5 to 9	576,895	12,284	144,715	59,871	338,882	100.0	2.1	25.1	10.4	58.7
Aged 10 to 14	604,628	11,171	157,882	46,629	368,250	100.0	1.8	26.1	7.7	60.9
Aged 15 to 17	370,763	7,864	98,272	24,422	227,221	100.0	2.1	26.5	6.6	61.3
Aged 18 to 19	255,023	4,517	70,030	19,606	155,220	100.0	1.8	27.5	7.7	60.9
Aged 20 to 24	601,228	12,764	141,383	57,988	368,952	100.0	2.1	23.5	9.6	61.4
Aged 25 to 29	588,088	13,503	125,932	72,679	363,621	100.0	2.3	21.4	12.4	61.8
Aged 30 to 34	611,849	17,779	126,125	73,999	381,567	100.0	2.9	20.6	12.1	62.4
Aged 35 to 44	1,330,032	29,736	283,604	90,860	903,034	100.0	2.2	21.3	6.8	67.9
Aged 45 to 54	1,269,316	20,260	269,879	41,911	913,869	100.0	1.6	21.3	3.3	72.0
Aged 55 to 64	974,151	12,752	173,738	15,812	758,370	100.0	1.3	17.8	1.6	77.8
Aged 65 to 74	576,276	6,060	92,925	6,773	462,927	100.0	1.1	16.1	1.2	80.3
Aged 75 to 84	373,398	1,958	52,931	2,335	312,066	100.0	0.5	14.2	0.6	83.6
Aged 85 or older	122,125	823	20,214	626	99,353	100.0	0.7	16.6	0.5	81.4
North Dakota	**635,867**	–	–	**9,332**	**575,108**	**100.0**	–	–	**1.5**	**90.4**
Under age 18	143,612	–	–	2,985	122,513	100.0	–	–	2.1	85.3
Under age 5	39,094	–	–	1,155	32,525	100.0	–	–	3.0	83.2
Aged 5 to 9	36,139	–	–	541	31,743	100.0	–	–	1.5	87.8
Aged 10 to 14	41,338	–	–	640	35,136	100.0	–	–	1.5	85.0
Aged 15 to 17	27,041	–	–	649	23,109	100.0	–	–	2.4	85.5
Aged 18 to 19	25,111	–	–	649	21,871	100.0	–	–	2.6	87.1
Aged 20 to 24	57,279	–	–	1,415	50,045	100.0	–	–	2.5	87.4
Aged 25 to 29	41,046	–	–	1,143	35,233	100.0	–	–	2.8	85.8
Aged 30 to 34	33,159	–	–	927	29,672	100.0	–	–	2.8	89.5
Aged 35 to 44	81,357	–	–	826	72,311	100.0	–	–	1.0	88.9
Aged 45 to 54	94,602	–	–	430	89,844	100.0	–	–	0.5	95.0
Aged 55 to 64	66,872	–	–	641	63,226	100.0	–	–	1.0	94.5
Aged 65 to 74	43,138	–	–	261	41,554	100.0	–	–	0.6	96.3
Aged 75 to 84	33,929	–	–	55	33,241	100.0	–	–	0.2	98.0
Aged 85 or older	15,762	–	–	0	15,598	100.0	–	–	0.0	99.0
Ohio	**11,478,006**	**175,000**	**1,357,343**	**265,762**	**9,506,469**	**100.0**	**1.5**	**11.8**	**2.3**	**82.8**
Under age 18	2,772,776	39,835	411,968	91,408	2,146,409	100.0	1.4	14.9	3.3	77.4
Under age 5	736,175	12,910	108,838	27,753	560,450	100.0	1.8	14.8	3.8	76.1
Aged 5 to 9	741,865	12,112	104,720	26,381	573,382	100.0	1.6	14.1	3.6	77.3
Aged 10 to 14	794,758	9,111	123,931	23,785	617,065	100.0	1.1	15.6	3.0	77.6
Aged 15 to 17	499,978	5,702	74,479	13,489	395,512	100.0	1.1	14.9	2.7	79.1
Aged 18 to 19	327,671	5,619	44,588	10,082	258,023	100.0	1.7	13.6	3.1	78.7
Aged 20 to 24	775,097	13,611	101,283	22,380	623,361	100.0	1.8	13.1	2.9	80.4
Aged 25 to 29	749,491	17,126	96,634	24,245	603,139	100.0	2.3	12.9	3.2	80.5
Aged 30 to 34	695,313	21,528	85,459	23,203	559,422	100.0	3.1	12.3	3.3	80.5
Aged 35 to 44	1,627,911	32,394	188,010	41,527	1,348,977	100.0	2.0	11.5	2.6	82.9
Aged 45 to 54	1,738,793	19,507	186,528	26,268	1,491,504	100.0	1.1	10.7	1.5	85.8
Aged 55 to 64	1,262,875	14,686	114,344	16,141	1,105,842	100.0	1.2	9.1	1.3	87.6
Aged 65 to 74	764,271	6,387	68,883	6,050	677,298	100.0	0.8	9.0	0.8	88.6
Aged 75 to 84	555,823	3,790	43,712	3,991	502,217	100.0	0.7	7.9	0.7	90.4
Aged 85 or older	207,985	517	15,934	467	190,277	100.0	0.2	7.7	0.2	91.5

	total	Asian	black	Hispanic	non-Hispanic white	total	Asian	black	Hispanic	non-Hispanic white
Oklahoma	**3,579,212**	**59,164**	**263,271**	**244,822**	**2,577,447**	**100.0%**	**1.7%**	**7.4%**	**6.8%**	**72.0%**
Under age 18	895,186	14,116	79,067	93,226	560,056	100.0	1.6	8.8	10.4	62.6
Under age 5	252,053	4,562	21,793	31,318	153,454	100.0	1.8	8.6	12.4	60.9
Aged 5 to 9	242,570	4,014	22,517	27,052	148,612	100.0	1.7	9.3	11.2	61.3
Aged 10 to 14	245,332	2,936	19,856	21,989	157,655	100.0	1.2	8.1	9.0	64.3
Aged 15 to 17	155,231	2,604	14,901	12,867	100,335	100.0	1.7	9.6	8.3	64.6
Aged 18 to 19	104,007	2,186	10,290	7,811	68,638	100.0	2.1	9.9	7.5	66.0
Aged 20 to 24	267,898	5,048	22,567	24,411	177,651	100.0	1.9	8.4	9.1	66.3
Aged 25 to 29	250,164	6,011	21,383	24,487	169,750	100.0	2.4	8.5	9.8	67.9
Aged 30 to 34	217,397	4,865	17,209	22,533	146,656	100.0	2.2	7.9	10.4	67.5
Aged 35 to 44	477,860	8,929	34,025	35,356	344,195	100.0	1.9	7.1	7.4	72.0
Aged 45 to 54	505,295	9,090	36,024	19,639	389,715	100.0	1.8	7.1	3.9	77.1
Aged 55 to 64	385,768	4,548	21,026	10,247	314,683	100.0	1.2	5.5	2.7	81.6
Aged 65 to 74	248,712	3,262	12,118	4,063	207,292	100.0	1.3	4.9	1.6	83.3
Aged 75 to 84	164,101	1,109	6,828	2,476	143,148	100.0	0.7	4.2	1.5	87.2
Aged 85 or older	62,824	0	2,734	573	55,663	100.0	0.0	4.4	0.9	88.6
Oregon	**3,700,758**	**135,746**	**63,631**	**379,034**	**2,989,235**	**100.0**	**3.7**	**1.7**	**10.2**	**80.8**
Under age 18	857,617	32,407	19,783	142,494	614,131	100.0	3.8	2.3	16.6	71.6
Under age 5	229,956	7,727	6,466	43,990	156,392	100.0	3.4	2.8	19.1	68.0
Aged 5 to 9	231,329	9,409	4,419	41,839	162,279	100.0	4.1	1.9	18.1	70.2
Aged 10 to 14	240,957	10,214	5,243	37,555	176,881	100.0	4.2	2.2	15.6	73.4
Aged 15 to 17	155,375	5,057	3,655	19,110	118,579	100.0	3.3	2.4	12.3	76.3
Aged 18 to 19	95,513	3,362	2,400	11,491	72,830	100.0	3.5	2.5	12.0	76.3
Aged 20 to 24	246,256	10,771	4,648	32,483	187,438	100.0	4.4	1.9	13.2	76.1
Aged 25 to 29	268,023	11,124	4,029	41,972	202,620	100.0	4.2	1.5	15.7	75.6
Aged 30 to 34	245,978	13,537	3,689	40,396	179,554	100.0	5.5	1.5	16.4	73.0
Aged 35 to 44	512,348	24,469	9,898	54,295	408,254	100.0	4.8	1.9	10.6	79.7
Aged 45 to 54	560,444	18,056	9,551	30,408	485,094	100.0	3.2	1.7	5.4	86.6
Aged 55 to 64	437,714	11,423	4,786	15,728	394,683	100.0	2.6	1.1	3.6	90.2
Aged 65 to 74	239,586	6,025	2,742	6,068	220,580	100.0	2.5	1.1	2.5	92.1
Aged 75 to 84	166,829	3,624	965	2,831	157,229	100.0	2.2	0.6	1.7	94.2
Aged 85 or older	70,450	948	1,140	868	66,822	100.0	1.3	1.6	1.2	94.9
Pennsylvania	**12,440,621**	**289,289**	**1,289,799**	**527,142**	**10,201,475**	**100.0**	**2.3**	**10.4**	**4.2**	**82.0**
Under age 18	2,807,534	66,270	380,701	187,125	2,104,029	100.0	2.4	13.6	6.7	74.9
Under age 5	724,450	20,621	100,842	57,255	523,165	100.0	2.8	13.9	7.9	72.2
Aged 5 to 9	742,644	19,650	96,885	50,136	556,820	100.0	2.6	13.0	6.8	75.0
Aged 10 to 14	809,077	16,252	110,524	50,774	613,048	100.0	2.0	13.7	6.3	75.8
Aged 15 to 17	531,363	9,747	72,450	28,960	410,996	100.0	1.8	13.6	5.5	77.3
Aged 18 to 19	378,258	11,241	49,461	21,324	289,921	100.0	3.0	13.1	5.6	76.6
Aged 20 to 24	822,970	24,453	95,255	43,324	651,193	100.0	3.0	11.6	5.3	79.1
Aged 25 to 29	720,977	24,311	85,181	46,231	556,120	100.0	3.4	11.8	6.4	77.1
Aged 30 to 34	717,916	30,130	80,486	43,281	558,457	100.0	4.2	11.2	6.0	77.8
Aged 35 to 44	1,777,911	53,122	189,175	79,738	1,445,590	100.0	3.0	10.6	4.5	81.3
Aged 45 to 54	1,918,048	37,023	172,850	53,408	1,643,326	100.0	1.9	9.0	2.8	85.7
Aged 55 to 64	1,413,773	23,483	110,539	30,937	1,243,304	100.0	1.7	7.8	2.2	87.9
Aged 65 to 74	887,342	12,711	67,490	12,933	790,349	100.0	1.4	7.6	1.5	89.1
Aged 75 to 84	723,983	5,793	43,808	6,941	665,428	100.0	0.8	6.1	1.0	91.9
Aged 85 or older	271,909	752	14,853	1,900	253,758	100.0	0.3	5.5	0.7	93.3

	total	Asian	black	Hispanic	non-Hispanic white	total	Asian	black	Hispanic	non-Hispanic white
Rhode Island	**1,067,610**	**29,406**	**54,396**	**117,708**	**842,726**	**100.0%**	**2.8%**	**5.1%**	**11.0%**	**78.9%**
Under age 18	237,447	7,214	16,538	42,141	162,120	100.0	3.0	7.0	17.7	68.3
Under age 5	61,798	2,249	4,029	12,382	39,161	100.0	3.6	6.5	20.0	63.4
Aged 5 to 9	62,571	1,599	4,124	12,930	40,835	100.0	2.6	6.6	20.7	65.3
Aged 10 to 14	69,382	2,059	5,091	10,289	50,302	100.0	3.0	7.3	14.8	72.5
Aged 15 to 17	43,696	1,307	3,294	6,540	31,822	100.0	3.0	7.5	15.0	72.8
Aged 18 to 19	37,453	1,640	2,346	4,341	27,751	100.0	4.4	6.3	11.6	74.1
Aged 20 to 24	79,726	3,491	4,965	10,408	59,092	100.0	4.4	6.2	13.1	74.1
Aged 25 to 29	66,345	3,014	4,129	10,267	47,335	100.0	4.5	6.2	15.5	71.3
Aged 30 to 34	63,506	2,028	4,571	9,847	46,271	100.0	3.2	7.2	15.5	72.9
Aged 35 to 44	159,682	4,509	7,952	18,631	125,822	100.0	2.8	5.0	11.7	78.8
Aged 45 to 54	159,950	3,181	7,169	11,569	135,453	100.0	2.0	4.5	7.2	84.7
Aged 55 to 64	116,057	1,928	3,832	5,919	102,883	100.0	1.7	3.3	5.1	88.6
Aged 65 to 74	67,112	1,362	1,453	2,838	60,512	100.0	2.0	2.2	4.2	90.2
Aged 75 to 84	54,909	989	1,199	1,201	51,337	100.0	1.8	2.2	2.2	93.5
Aged 85 or older	25,423	50	242	546	24,150	100.0	0.2	1.0	2.1	95.0
South Carolina	**4,321,249**	**46,939**	**1,237,900**	**148,632**	**2,823,274**	**100.0**	**1.1**	**28.6**	**3.4**	**65.3**
Under age 18	1,038,866	10,994	347,823	48,584	600,960	100.0	1.1	33.5	4.7	57.8
Under age 5	284,708	2,808	90,177	19,395	161,546	100.0	1.0	31.7	6.8	56.7
Aged 5 to 9	275,178	2,833	90,594	12,803	160,577	100.0	1.0	32.9	4.7	58.4
Aged 10 to 14	290,615	3,586	99,550	10,921	169,019	100.0	1.2	34.3	3.8	58.2
Aged 15 to 17	188,365	1,767	67,502	5,465	109,818	100.0	0.9	35.8	2.9	58.3
Aged 18 to 19	135,837	619	50,708	5,035	77,634	100.0	0.5	37.3	3.7	57.2
Aged 20 to 24	300,802	3,583	100,241	16,105	176,810	100.0	1.2	33.3	5.4	58.8
Aged 25 to 29	279,729	3,595	83,431	17,329	172,059	100.0	1.3	29.8	6.2	61.5
Aged 30 to 34	273,747	6,919	71,905	17,848	172,632	100.0	2.5	26.3	6.5	63.1
Aged 35 to 44	619,503	8,395	178,461	25,114	401,453	100.0	1.4	28.8	4.1	64.8
Aged 45 to 54	618,659	5,352	172,761	10,754	422,673	100.0	0.9	27.9	1.7	68.3
Aged 55 to 64	500,251	3,724	117,395	4,569	370,179	100.0	0.7	23.5	0.9	74.0
Aged 65 to 74	301,498	3,087	64,317	2,231	230,265	100.0	1.0	21.3	0.7	76.4
Aged 75 to 84	188,250	534	37,168	697	148,860	100.0	0.3	19.7	0.4	79.1
Aged 85 or older	64,107	137	13,690	366	49,749	100.0	0.2	21.4	0.6	77.6
South Dakota	**781,919**	**–**	**–**	**15,544**	**676,671**	**100.0**	**–**	**–**	**2.0**	**86.5**
Under age 18	193,977	–	–	5,804	151,369	100.0	–	–	3.0	78.0
Under age 5	53,701	–	–	1,601	41,554	100.0	–	–	3.0	77.4
Aged 5 to 9	49,689	–	–	1,644	38,470	100.0	–	–	3.3	77.4
Aged 10 to 14	56,911	–	–	2,031	43,379	100.0	–	–	3.6	76.2
Aged 15 to 17	33,676	–	–	528	27,966	100.0	–	–	1.6	83.0
Aged 18 to 19	23,228	–	–	335	18,795	100.0	–	–	1.4	80.9
Aged 20 to 24	59,477	–	–	1,751	50,241	100.0	–	–	2.9	84.5
Aged 25 to 29	50,687	–	–	1,502	43,145	100.0	–	–	3.0	85.1
Aged 30 to 34	42,053	–	–	1,191	35,250	100.0	–	–	2.8	83.8
Aged 35 to 44	102,730	–	–	1,976	89,354	100.0	–	–	1.9	87.0
Aged 45 to 54	114,930	–	–	1,643	104,130	100.0	–	–	1.4	90.6
Aged 55 to 64	83,198	–	–	630	77,975	100.0	–	–	0.8	93.7
Aged 65 to 74	53,237	–	–	421	49,789	100.0	–	–	0.8	93.5
Aged 75 to 84	40,502	–	–	224	39,495	100.0	–	–	0.6	97.5
Aged 85 or older	17,900	–	–	67	17,128	100.0	–	–	0.4	95.7

	total	Asian	black	Hispanic	non-Hispanic white	total	Asian	black	Hispanic	non-Hispanic white
Tennessee	**6,038,803**	**76,208**	**1,011,726**	**187,747**	**4,677,757**	**100.0%**	**1.3%**	**16.8%**	**3.1%**	**77.5%**
Under age 18	1,447,050	20,364	304,005	67,237	1,018,434	100.0	1.4	21.0	4.6	70.4
Under age 5	399,006	6,335	80,376	27,264	273,256	100.0	1.6	20.1	6.8	68.5
Aged 5 to 9	386,039	6,430	77,626	17,189	273,522	100.0	1.7	20.1	4.5	70.9
Aged 10 to 14	406,769	5,074	89,533	15,986	287,458	100.0	1.2	22.0	3.9	70.7
Aged 15 to 17	255,236	2,525	56,470	6,798	184,198	100.0	1.0	22.1	2.7	72.2
Aged 18 to 19	162,348	2,131	35,995	4,962	117,219	100.0	1.3	22.2	3.1	72.2
Aged 20 to 24	391,579	4,271	78,794	18,249	285,884	100.0	1.1	20.1	4.7	73.0
Aged 25 to 29	432,397	7,007	79,656	24,995	316,960	100.0	1.6	18.4	5.8	73.3
Aged 30 to 34	397,266	8,630	69,777	20,740	293,918	100.0	2.2	17.6	5.2	74.0
Aged 35 to 44	877,946	14,089	146,608	25,828	681,174	100.0	1.6	16.7	2.9	77.6
Aged 45 to 54	877,038	9,649	135,559	13,875	706,016	100.0	1.1	15.5	1.6	80.5
Aged 55 to 64	686,086	6,095	82,611	6,709	584,044	100.0	0.9	12.0	1.0	85.1
Aged 65 to 74	414,416	2,534	43,845	2,735	361,979	100.0	0.6	10.6	0.7	87.3
Aged 75 to 84	259,230	1,179	23,915	1,893	230,836	100.0	0.5	9.2	0.7	89.0
Aged 85 or older	93,447	259	10,961	524	81,293	100.0	0.3	11.7	0.6	87.0
Texas	**23,507,783**	**787,208**	**2,718,515**	**8,385,118**	**11,309,011**	**100.0**	**3.3**	**11.6**	**35.7**	**48.1**
Under age 18	6,502,854	194,280	812,389	2,923,046	2,456,574	100.0	3.0	12.5	45.0	37.8
Under age 5	1,922,227	57,522	222,765	942,451	663,592	100.0	3.0	11.6	49.0	34.5
Aged 5 to 9	1,763,310	56,807	216,878	804,292	653,556	100.0	3.2	12.3	45.6	37.1
Aged 10 to 14	1,755,999	50,427	230,225	751,967	693,554	100.0	2.9	13.1	42.8	39.5
Aged 15 to 17	1,061,318	29,524	142,521	424,336	445,872	100.0	2.8	13.4	40.0	42.0
Aged 18 to 19	708,816	20,391	94,092	275,256	309,213	100.0	2.9	13.3	38.8	43.6
Aged 20 to 24	1,744,419	52,415	218,408	708,357	747,330	100.0	3.0	12.5	40.6	42.8
Aged 25 to 29	1,747,112	66,758	209,703	750,449	702,243	100.0	3.8	12.0	43.0	40.2
Aged 30 to 34	1,686,303	81,940	195,635	715,472	672,211	100.0	4.9	11.6	42.4	39.9
Aged 35 to 44	3,447,637	146,131	410,025	1,212,641	1,640,072	100.0	4.2	11.9	35.2	47.6
Aged 45 to 54	3,171,706	107,926	369,583	850,497	1,802,764	100.0	3.4	11.7	26.8	56.8
Aged 55 to 64	2,169,494	67,874	214,420	492,285	1,369,527	100.0	3.1	9.9	22.7	63.1
Aged 65 to 74	1,243,160	34,344	111,512	261,338	824,608	100.0	2.8	9.0	21.0	66.3
Aged 75 to 84	803,994	12,301	62,719	155,617	566,888	100.0	1.5	7.8	19.4	70.5
Aged 85 or older	282,288	2,848	20,029	40,160	217,581	100.0	1.0	7.1	14.2	77.1
Utah	**2,550,063**	**49,079**	**22,742**	**286,113**	**2,112,440**	**100.0**	**1.9**	**0.9**	**11.2**	**82.8**
Under age 18	792,172	11,642	8,326	109,642	626,978	100.0	1.5	1.1	13.8	79.1
Under age 5	247,167	3,126	2,681	36,140	194,537	100.0	1.3	1.1	14.6	78.7
Aged 5 to 9	216,550	3,262	2,173	31,490	169,719	100.0	1.5	1.0	14.5	78.4
Aged 10 to 14	205,303	3,345	2,305	27,497	162,988	100.0	1.6	1.1	13.4	79.4
Aged 15 to 17	123,152	1,909	1,167	14,515	99,734	100.0	1.6	0.9	11.8	81.0
Aged 18 to 19	83,962	1,984	713	9,574	67,678	100.0	2.4	0.8	11.4	80.6
Aged 20 to 24	236,368	4,090	2,379	25,507	197,865	100.0	1.7	1.0	10.8	83.7
Aged 25 to 29	232,726	3,679	1,758	30,017	190,389	100.0	1.6	0.8	12.9	81.8
Aged 30 to 34	173,977	5,804	2,075	26,767	133,179	100.0	3.3	1.2	15.4	76.5
Aged 35 to 44	311,641	8,554	2,716	40,540	251,496	100.0	2.7	0.9	13.0	80.7
Aged 45 to 54	294,153	5,848	2,664	23,472	255,819	100.0	2.0	0.9	8.0	87.0
Aged 55 to 64	201,104	3,536	1,271	12,527	180,349	100.0	1.8	0.6	6.2	89.7
Aged 65 to 74	117,551	1,919	433	4,976	108,659	100.0	1.6	0.4	4.2	92.4
Aged 75 to 84	78,755	1,835	308	2,269	73,611	100.0	2.3	0.4	2.9	93.5
Aged 85 or older	27,654	188	99	822	26,417	100.0	0.7	0.4	3.0	95.5

	total	Asian	black	Hispanic	non-Hispanic white	total	Asian	black	Hispanic	non-Hispanic white
Vermont	**623,908**	**5,693**	**–**	**6,644**	**596,638**	**100.0%**	**0.9%**	**–**	**1.1%**	**95.6%**
Under age 18	133,904	1,615	–	1,978	125,826	100.0	1.2	–	1.5	94.0
Under age 5	33,014	691	–	582	30,796	100.0	2.1	–	1.8	93.3
Aged 5 to 9	32,899	353	–	283	31,177	100.0	1.1	–	0.9	94.8
Aged 10 to 14	40,434	205	–	710	38,197	100.0	0.5	–	1.8	94.5
Aged 15 to 17	27,557	366	–	403	25,656	100.0	1.3	–	1.5	93.1
Aged 18 to 19	20,564	197	–	467	18,907	100.0	1.0	–	2.3	91.9
Aged 20 to 24	42,510	622	–	703	39,389	100.0	1.5	–	1.7	92.7
Aged 25 to 29	36,529	661	–	736	34,156	100.0	1.8	–	2.0	93.5
Aged 30 to 34	33,473	372	–	271	32,269	100.0	1.1	–	0.8	96.4
Aged 35 to 44	90,578	1,009	–	981	86,871	100.0	1.1	–	1.1	95.9
Aged 45 to 54	104,478	589	–	723	100,967	100.0	0.6	–	0.7	96.6
Aged 55 to 64	78,927	431	–	384	77,044	100.0	0.5	–	0.5	97.6
Aged 65 to 74	42,743	147	–	215	41,591	100.0	0.3	–	0.5	97.3
Aged 75 to 84	29,416	0	–	121	28,947	100.0	0.0	–	0.4	98.4
Aged 85 or older	10,786	50	–	65	10,671	100.0	0.5	–	0.6	98.9
Virginia	**7,642,884**	**365,515**	**1,496,076**	**470,871**	**5,167,028**	**100.0**	**4.8**	**19.6**	**6.2**	**67.6**
Under age 18	1,805,553	80,654	406,216	147,499	1,103,876	100.0	4.5	22.5	8.2	61.1
Under age 5	503,491	24,542	106,707	53,824	296,576	100.0	4.9	21.2	10.7	58.9
Aged 5 to 9	479,241	21,553	107,880	39,192	291,563	100.0	4.5	22.5	8.2	60.8
Aged 10 to 14	506,389	22,293	117,395	33,952	316,396	100.0	4.4	23.2	6.7	62.5
Aged 15 to 17	316,432	12,266	74,234	20,531	199,341	100.0	3.9	23.5	6.5	63.0
Aged 18 to 19	231,887	10,110	54,113	15,134	147,068	100.0	4.4	23.3	6.5	63.4
Aged 20 to 24	536,451	24,504	117,487	47,432	336,736	100.0	4.6	21.9	8.8	62.8
Aged 25 to 29	510,868	28,016	102,734	55,224	315,386	100.0	5.5	20.1	10.8	61.7
Aged 30 to 34	503,234	41,272	94,790	46,712	312,325	100.0	8.2	18.8	9.3	62.1
Aged 35 to 44	1,192,313	71,443	237,358	77,368	791,899	100.0	6.0	19.9	6.5	66.4
Aged 45 to 54	1,141,333	50,769	217,423	46,292	812,810	100.0	4.4	19.0	4.1	71.2
Aged 55 to 64	835,231	33,032	132,152	20,582	641,780	100.0	4.0	15.8	2.5	76.8
Aged 65 to 74	475,451	17,834	73,751	9,305	370,622	100.0	3.8	15.5	2.0	78.0
Aged 75 to 84	301,207	6,814	44,932	4,078	243,156	100.0	2.3	14.9	1.4	80.7
Aged 85 or older	109,356	1,067	15,120	1,245	91,370	100.0	1.0	13.8	1.1	83.6
Washington	**6,395,798**	**423,976**	**217,868**	**580,027**	**4,886,203**	**100.0**	**6.6**	**3.4**	**9.1**	**76.4**
Under age 18	1,527,876	90,620	65,170	221,991	1,036,334	100.0	5.9	4.3	14.5	67.8
Under age 5	406,816	24,536	17,306	70,808	259,563	100.0	6.0	4.3	17.4	63.8
Aged 5 to 9	409,095	23,870	19,162	64,449	269,371	100.0	5.8	4.7	15.8	65.8
Aged 10 to 14	437,285	26,291	17,397	56,060	307,869	100.0	6.0	4.0	12.8	70.4
Aged 15 to 17	274,680	15,923	11,305	30,674	199,531	100.0	5.8	4.1	11.2	72.6
Aged 18 to 19	180,368	13,602	7,448	20,438	125,063	100.0	7.5	4.1	11.3	69.3
Aged 20 to 24	433,972	29,761	17,623	49,115	312,131	100.0	6.9	4.1	11.3	71.9
Aged 25 to 29	458,484	34,884	18,007	59,329	326,173	100.0	7.6	3.9	12.9	71.1
Aged 30 to 34	430,157	43,144	16,042	54,025	297,163	100.0	10.0	3.7	12.6	69.1
Aged 35 to 44	948,214	74,135	34,350	84,590	722,382	100.0	7.8	3.6	8.9	76.2
Aged 45 to 54	970,799	61,923	30,868	48,132	800,085	100.0	6.4	3.2	5.0	82.4
Aged 55 to 64	709,212	38,593	16,172	24,292	610,813	100.0	5.4	2.3	3.4	86.1
Aged 65 to 74	379,702	22,118	7,063	11,486	330,424	100.0	5.8	1.9	3.0	87.0
Aged 75 to 84	254,060	11,659	4,106	5,346	229,362	100.0	4.6	1.6	2.1	90.3
Aged 85 or older	102,954	3,537	1,019	1,283	96,273	100.0	3.4	1.0	1.2	93.5

	total	Asian	black	Hispanic	non-Hispanic white	total	Asian	black	Hispanic	non-Hispanic white
West Virginia	**1,818,470**	**10,479**	**58,693**	**14,383**	**1,711,605**	**100.0%**	**0.6%**	**3.2%**	**0.8%**	**94.1%**
Under age 18	390,221	1,834	12,245	5,298	360,029	100.0	0.5	3.1	1.4	92.3
Under age 5	104,429	681	2,851	1,602	96,788	100.0	0.7	2.7	1.5	92.7
Aged 5 to 9	101,776	609	3,644	1,435	93,202	100.0	0.6	3.6	1.4	91.6
Aged 10 to 14	112,468	303	3,654	1,032	103,637	100.0	0.3	3.2	0.9	92.1
Aged 15 to 17	71,548	241	2,096	1,229	66,402	100.0	0.3	2.9	1.7	92.8
Aged 18 to 19	49,141	173	1,905	1,013	44,937	100.0	0.4	3.9	2.1	91.4
Aged 20 to 24	116,175	938	4,811	779	108,294	100.0	0.8	4.1	0.7	93.2
Aged 25 to 29	117,716	806	4,022	1,420	110,546	100.0	0.7	3.4	1.2	93.9
Aged 30 to 34	106,083	618	4,657	577	99,482	100.0	0.6	4.4	0.5	93.8
Aged 35 to 44	249,536	1,981	7,843	2,224	235,102	100.0	0.8	3.1	0.9	94.2
Aged 45 to 54	279,544	1,428	10,108	860	264,822	100.0	0.5	3.6	0.3	94.7
Aged 55 to 64	230,937	1,611	6,179	1,041	219,999	100.0	0.7	2.7	0.5	95.3
Aged 65 to 74	143,894	808	2,390	715	138,983	100.0	0.6	1.7	0.5	96.6
Aged 75 to 84	101,907	282	2,892	348	97,807	100.0	0.3	2.8	0.3	96.0
Aged 85 or older	33,316	0	1,641	108	31,604	100.0	0.0	4.9	0.3	94.9
Wisconsin	**5,556,506**	**110,778**	**328,376**	**256,304**	**4,755,716**	**100.0**	**2.0**	**5.9**	**4.6**	**85.6**
Under age 18	1,314,943	36,828	115,200	93,402	1,025,515	100.0	2.8	8.8	7.1	78.0
Under age 5	351,702	9,871	31,387	29,544	267,223	100.0	2.8	8.9	8.4	76.0
Aged 5 to 9	345,873	9,547	31,822	26,896	264,898	100.0	2.8	9.2	7.8	76.6
Aged 10 to 14	375,856	11,244	31,394	24,956	297,219	100.0	3.0	8.4	6.6	79.1
Aged 15 to 17	241,512	6,166	20,597	12,006	196,175	100.0	2.6	8.5	5.0	81.2
Aged 18 to 19	159,152	4,054	10,856	8,963	131,801	100.0	2.5	6.8	5.6	82.8
Aged 20 to 24	399,780	10,048	26,252	22,492	331,792	100.0	2.5	6.6	5.6	83.0
Aged 25 to 29	360,325	9,346	28,306	27,552	288,244	100.0	2.6	7.9	7.6	80.0
Aged 30 to 34	337,112	11,268	23,664	25,891	270,254	100.0	3.3	7.0	7.7	80.2
Aged 35 to 44	807,871	16,865	43,250	37,697	695,532	100.0	2.1	5.4	4.7	86.1
Aged 45 to 54	856,132	10,568	39,989	22,032	771,832	100.0	1.2	4.7	2.6	90.2
Aged 55 to 64	599,318	7,589	22,302	10,452	553,283	100.0	1.3	3.7	1.7	92.3
Aged 65 to 74	356,158	2,621	11,362	5,332	334,482	100.0	0.7	3.2	1.5	93.9
Aged 75 to 84	259,719	1,175	5,497	2,112	249,877	100.0	0.5	2.1	0.8	96.2
Aged 85 or older	105,996	416	1,698	379	103,104	100.0	0.4	1.6	0.4	97.3
Wyoming	**515,004**	–	–	**35,732**	**453,251**	**100.0**	–	–	**6.9**	**88.0**
Under age 18	120,930	–	–	11,538	101,699	100.0	–	–	9.5	84.1
Under age 5	34,128	–	–	3,632	27,701	100.0	–	–	10.6	81.2
Aged 5 to 9	31,557	–	–	3,711	26,419	100.0	–	–	11.8	83.7
Aged 10 to 14	32,883	–	–	2,469	28,048	100.0	–	–	7.5	85.3
Aged 15 to 17	22,362	–	–	1,726	19,531	100.0	–	–	7.7	87.3
Aged 18 to 19	14,802	–	–	828	12,870	100.0	–	–	5.6	86.9
Aged 20 to 24	39,874	–	–	2,651	34,263	100.0	–	–	6.6	85.9
Aged 25 to 29	35,505	–	–	3,214	29,832	100.0	–	–	9.1	84.0
Aged 30 to 34	30,148	–	–	2,319	25,924	100.0	–	–	7.7	86.0
Aged 35 to 44	65,430	–	–	4,620	57,979	100.0	–	–	7.1	88.6
Aged 45 to 54	84,698	–	–	5,457	75,902	100.0	–	–	6.4	89.6
Aged 55 to 64	61,987	–	–	3,571	55,813	100.0	–	–	5.8	90.0
Aged 65 to 74	32,630	–	–	793	31,124	100.0	–	–	2.4	95.4
Aged 75 to 84	21,573	–	–	535	20,837	100.0	–	–	2.5	96.6
Aged 85 or older	7,427	–	–	206	7,008	100.0	–	–	2.8	94.4

Note: Numbers will not add to total because each race includes only those who identified themselves as being of the race alone, not all races are shown, and Hispanics may be of any race. Non-Hispanic whites are those who identified themselves as being white alone and not Hispanic. "–" means sample is too small to make a reliable estimate.
Source: Bureau of the Census, 2006 American Community Survey, Internet site http://factfinder.census.gov/home/saff/main .html?_lang=en; calculations by New Strategist

Appendix 2

How to Get Local Demographics from the American Community Survey

If you want to explore the local demographics of your market, there is no better source of data than the American Community Survey. An ongoing nationwide survey of 250,000 households, the ACS provides detailed demographic data at the community level. Designed to replace the census "long form" questionnaire in the 2010 census, the ACS began in 2000. It includes more than 60 questions that formerly appeared on the long form, such as ones asking about language spoken at home, income, and education. ACS data are available for areas as small as census tracts.

The ACS is designed to give policymakers, researchers, and businesses an up-to-date look at how communities are changing. The census long form had been providing demographic and socioeconomic information about Americans at the local level for many decades, but because the census long form was administered only once every ten years, the local data it provided was soon out of date. The ACS is producing that important community data every year instead of every decade.

The ACS produces estimates of demographic and socioeconomic characteristics for states, cities, counties, metropolitan areas, and populations of 65,000 or more every year. It provides data for smaller areas every three to five years as it builds a sufficient sample size to produce reliable local area data. For areas with 20,000 to 65,000 people, data are available every three years. For rural areas, city neighborhoods, and populations of less than 20,000, the ACS produces data every five years. These three- or five-year averages can be updated every year, allowing researchers to measure changes over time for small areas.

The ACS provides a variety of data on children. Not only will it tell you how many children live in a given area by age, but it will also reveal their race, family type, family income, school enrollment status, language spoken at home, citizenship status, disability status, and so on.

If you need to know the demographics of children in a local market, there is no better place to go than the ACS. Once you master the variety of ways to extract data from this massive online database, you will be able to produce up-to-date estimates of the demographics of the children's market at the national, state, metropolitan area, or community level. Here is a brief rundown on how to get information online from the ACS:

1. Go to the ACS web site at http://www.census.gov/acs/www/

2. Click on "American Factfinder."

3. On the next page click the "Get Data" link under the American Community Survey heading.

4. On the next page, click on the American Community Survey "Subject Tables" link. On the next page, choose your geography. Once chosen, a list of subject tables will appear, one section of which is devoted to children. Click on the "Children Characteristics" table for the latest numbers for your chosen geography.

5. If you would rather create your own tables of data, then click on "Custom Table" rather than "Subject Tables" in the above description and follow the prompts to examine hundreds of possible tabulations of ACS data for your requested geography.

Glossary

adjusted for inflation Income or a change in income that has been adjusted for the rise in the cost of living, or the consumer price index (CPI-U-RS).

American Community Survey The ACS is an on-going nationwide survey of 250,000 households per month, providing detailed demographic data at the community level. Designed to replace the census long-form questionnaire, the ACS includes more than 60 questions that formerly appeared on the long form, such as language spoken at home, income, and education. ACS data are available for areas as small as census tracts.

American Housing Survey The AHS collects national and metropolitan-level data on the nation's housing, including apartments, single-family homes, and mobile homes. The nationally representative survey, with a sample of 55,000 homes, is conducted by the Census Bureau for the Department of Housing and Urban Development every other year.

American Indians In this book, American Indians include Alaska Natives (Eskimos and Aleuts) unless those groups are shown separately.

American Time Use Survey Under contract with the Bureau of Labor Statistics, the Census Bureau collects ATUS information, revealing how people spend their time. The ATUS sample is drawn from U.S. households completing their final month of interviews for the Current Population Survey. One individual from each selected household is chosen to participate in ATUS. Respondents are interviewed by telephone about their time use during the previous 24 hours. About 40,500 households are included in the sample each year.

Asian The term "Asian" includes Native Hawaiians and other Pacific Islanders unless those groups are shown separately.

baby boom Americans born between 1946 and 1964.

baby bust Americans born between 1965 and 1976, also known as Generation X.

Behavioral Risk Factor Surveillance System The BRFSS is a collaborative project of the Centers for Disease Control and Prevention and U.S. states and territories. It is an ongoing data collection program designed to measure behavioral risk factors in the adult population aged 18 or older. All 50 states, three territories, and the District of Columbia take part in the survey, making the BRFSS the primary source of information on the health-related behaviors of Americans.

black The black racial category includes those who identified themselves as "black" or "African American."

Consumer Expenditure Survey The CEX is an ongoing study of the day-to-day spending of American households administered by the Bureau of Labor Statistics. The CEX includes an interview survey and a diary survey. The average spending figures shown in this book are the integrated data from both the diary and interview components of the survey. Two separate, nationally representative samples are used for the interview and diary surveys. For the interview survey, about 7,500 consumer units are interviewed on a rotating panel basis each quarter for five consecutive quarters. For the diary survey, 7,500 consumer units keep weekly diaries of spending for two consecutive weeks.

consumer unit *(on spending tables only)* For convenience, the term consumer unit and household are used interchangeably in the Spending chapter of this book, although consumer units are somewhat different from the Census Bureau's households. Consumer units are all related members of a household, or financially independent members of a household. A household may include more than one consumer unit.

Current Population Survey The CPS is a nationally representative survey of the civilian noninstitutional population aged 15 or older. It is taken monthly by the Census Bureau for the Bureau of Labor Statistics, collecting information from more than 50,000 households on employment and unemployment. In March of each year, the survey includes the Annual Social and Economic Supplement (formerly called the Annual Demographic Survey), which is the source of most national data on the characteristics of Americans, such as educational attainment, living arrangements, and incomes.

disability The National Health Interview Survey estimates the number of people aged 18 or older who have difficulty in physical functioning, probing whether respondents could perform nine activities by themselves without using special equipment. The categories are walking a quarter mile; standing for two hours; sitting for two hours; walking up ten steps without resting; stooping, bending, kneeling; reaching over one's head; grasping or handling small objects; carrying a ten-pound object; and pushing / pulling a large object. Adults who reported that any of these activities was very difficult or they could not do it at all were defined as having physical difficulties.

dual-earner couple A married couple in which both the husband and wife are in the labor force.

earnings A type of income, earnings is the amount of money a person receives from his or her job. See also Income.

employed All civilians who did any work as a paid employee or farmer / self-employed worker, or who worked 15 hours or more as an unpaid farm worker or in a family-owned business, during the reference period. All those who have jobs but who are temporarily absent from their jobs due to illness, bad weather, vacation, labor management dispute, or personal reasons are considered employed.

expenditure The transaction cost including excise and sales taxes of goods and services acquired during the survey period. The full cost of each purchase is recorded even though full payment may not have been made at the date of purchase. Average expenditure figures may be artificially low for infrequently purchased items such as cars because figures are calculated using all consumer units within a demographic segment rather than just purchasers. Expenditure estimates include money spent on gifts for others.

family A group of two or more people (one of whom is the householder) related by birth, marriage, or adoption and living in the same household.

family household A household maintained by a householder who lives with one or more people related to him or her by blood, marriage, or adoption.

female/male householder A woman or man who maintains a household without a spouse present. May head family or nonfamily households.

foreign-born population People who are not U.S. citizens at birth.

full-time employment Full-time is 35 or more hours of work per week during a majority of the weeks worked.

full-time, year-round Indicates 50 or more weeks of full-time employment during the previous calendar year.

General Social Survey The GSS is a biennial survey of the attitudes of Americans taken by the University of Chicago's National Opinion Research Center. NORC conducts the GSS through face-to-face interviews with an independently drawn, representative sample of 1,500 to 3,000 noninstitutionalized English-speaking people aged 18 or older who live in the United States.

generation X Americans born between 1965 and 1976, also known as the baby-bust generation.

Hispanic Because Hispanic is an ethnic origin rather than a race, Hispanics may be of any race. While most Hispanics are white, there are black, Asian, American Indian, and even Native Hawaiian Hispanics.

household All the persons who occupy a housing unit. A household includes the related family members and all the unrelated persons, if any, such as lodgers, foster children, wards, or employees who share the housing unit. A person living alone is counted as a household. A group of unrelated people who share a housing unit as roommates or unmarried partners is also counted as a household. Households do not include group quarters such as college dormitories, prisons, or nursing homes.

household, race/ethnicity of Households are categorized according to the race or ethnicity of the householder only.

householder The householder is the person (or one of the persons) in whose name the housing unit is owned or rented or, if there is no such person, any adult member. With married couples, the householder may be either the husband or wife. The householder is the reference person for the household.

householder, age of The age of the householder is used to categorize households into age groups such as those used in this book. Married couples, for example, are classified according to the age of either the husband or wife, depending on which one identified him or herself as the householder.

housing unit A housing unit is a house, an apartment, a group of rooms, or a single room occupied or intended for occupancy as separate living quarters. Separate living quarters are those in which the occupants do not live and eat with any other persons in the structure and that have direct access from the outside of the building or through a common hall that is used or intended for use by the occupants of another unit or by the general public. The occupants may be a single family, one person living alone, two or more families living together, or any other group of related or unrelated persons who share living arrangements.

Housing Vacancy Survey The HVS is a supplement to the Current Population Survey, providing quarterly and annual data on rental and homeowner vacancy rates, characteristics of units available for occupancy, and homeownership rates by age, household type, region, state, and metropolitan area. The Current Population Survey sample includes 51,000 occupied housing units and 9,000 vacant units.

housing value The respondent's estimate of how much his or her house and lot would sell for if it were for sale.

immigration The relatively permanent movement (change of residence) of people into the country of reference.

in-migration The relatively permanent movement (change of residence) of people into a subnational geographic entity, such as a region, division, state, metropolitan area, or county.

income Money received in the preceding calendar year by each person aged 15 or older from each of the following sources: 1) earnings from longest job or self-employment), 2) earnings from jobs other than longest job, 3) unemployment compensation, 4) workers' compensation, 5) Social Security, 6) Supplemental Security income, 7) public assistance, 8) veterans' payments, 9) survivor benefits, 10) disability benefits, 11) retirement pensions, 12) interest, 13) dividends, 14) rents and royalties or estates and trusts, 15) educational assistance, 16) alimony, 17) child support, 18) financial assistance from outside the household, and other periodic income. Income is reported in several ways in this book. Household income is the combined income of all household members. Income of persons is all income accruing to a person from all sources. Earnings are the money a person receives from his or her job.

industry Refers to the industry in which a person worked longest in the preceding calendar year.

job tenure The length of time a person has been employed continuously by the same employer.

labor force The labor force tables in this book show the civilian labor force only. The labor force includes both the employed and the unemployed (people who are looking for work). People are counted as in the labor force if they were working or looking for work during the reference week in which the Census Bureau fields the Current Population Survey.

labor force participation rate The percent of the civilian noninstitutional population that is in the civilian labor force, which includes both the employed and the unemployed.

married couples with or without children under age 18 Refers to married couples with or without own children under age 18 living in the same household. Couples without children under age 18 may be parents of grown children who live elsewhere, or they could be childless couples.

median The median is the amount that divides the population or households into two equal portions: one below and one above the median. Medians can be calculated for income, age, and many other characteristics.

median income The amount that divides the income distribution into two equal groups, half having incomes above the median, half having incomes below the median. The medians for households or families are based on all households or families. The median for persons are based on all persons aged 15 or older with income.

metropolitan statistical area The general concept of a metropolitan area is a large population nucleus with adjacent communities having a high degree of social and economic integration with the core. The Office of Management and Budget defines the nation's metropolitan statistical areas. In general, they must include a city or urbanized area with 50,000 or more inhabitants and a total population of 100,000 or more. The county (or counties) that contains the largest city is the "central county" (counties), along with any adjacent counties that are socially and economically integrated with the central county (or counties). In New England, MSAs are defined in terms of cities and towns rather than counties.

millennial generation Americans born between 1977 and 1994.

mobility status People are classified according to their mobility status on the basis of a comparison between their place of residence at the time of the March Current Population Survey and their place of residence in March of the previous year. Nonmovers are people living in the same house at the end of the period as at the beginning of the period. Movers are people living in a different house at the end of the period than at the beginning of the period. Movers from abroad are either citizens or aliens whose place of residence is outside the United States at the beginning of the period, that is, in an outlying area under the jurisdiction of the United States or in a foreign country. The mobility status of children is fully allocated from the mother if she is in the household; otherwise it is allocated from the householder.

National Ambulatory Medical Care Survey The NAMCS is an annual survey of visits to nonfederally employed office-based physicians who are primarily engaged in direct patient care. Data are collected from physicians rather than patients, with each physician assigned a one-week reporting period. During the week, the physician or office staff record a systematic random sample of visit characteristics.

National Compensation Survey The Bureau of Labor Statistics' NCS examines the incidence and detailed provisions of selected employee benefit plans in small, medium, and large private establishments, and state and local governments. Each year BLS economists visit a representative sample of establishments across the country, asking questions about the establishment, its employees, and their benefits.

National Crime Victimization Survey The NCVS collects data each year on nonfatal crimes against people aged 12 or older, reported and not reported to the police, from a nationally representative sample of 42,000 households and 76,000 persons in the United States. The NCVS provides information about victims, offenders, and criminal offenses.

National Health and Nutrition Examination Survey The NHANES is a continuous survey of a representative sample of the U.S. civilian noninstitutionalized population. Respondents are interviewed at home about their health and nutrition, and the interview is followed up by a physical examination that measures such things as height and weight in mobile examination centers.

National Health Interview Survey The NHIS is a continuing nationwide sample survey of the civilian noninstitutional population of the U.S. conducted by the Census Bureau for the National Center for Health Statistics. In interviews each year, data are collected from more than 100,000 people about their illnesses, injuries, impairments, chronic and acute conditions, activity limitations, and use of health services.

National Hospital Ambulatory Medical Care Survey The NHAMCS, sponsored by the National Center for Health Statistics, is an annual national probability sample survey of visits to emergency departments and outpatient departments at non-Federal, short stay and general hospitals. Hospital staff collect data from patient records.

National Household Education Survey The NHES, sponsored by the National Center for Education Statistics, provides descriptive data on the educational activities of the U.S. population, including after-school care and adult education. The NHES is a system of telephone surveys of a representative sample of 45,000 to 60,000 households in the U.S.

Native Hawaiian and other Pacific Islander The 2000 census identified this group for the first time as a separate racial category from Asians. In most survey data, however, the population is included with Asians.

net migration Net migration is the result of subtracting out-migration from in-migration for an area. Another way to derive net migration is to subtract natural increase (births minus deaths) from total population change in an area.

nonfamily household A household maintained by a householder who lives alone or who lives with people to whom he or she is not related.

nonfamily householder A householder who lives alone or with nonrelatives.

non-Hispanic People who do not identify themselves as Hispanic are classified as non-Hispanic. Non-Hispanics may be of any race.

non-Hispanic white People who identify their race as white alone and who do not indicate an Hispanic origin.

nonmetropolitan area Counties that are not classified as metropolitan areas.

occupation Occupational classification is based on the kind of work a person did at his or her job during the previous calendar year. If a person changed jobs during the year, the data refer to the occupation of the job held the longest during that year.

occupied housing units A housing unit is classified as occupied if a person or group of people is living in it or if the occupants are only temporarily absent—on vacation, example. By definition, the count of occupied housing units is the same as the count of households.

outside principal cities The portion of a metropolitan county or counties that falls outside of the principal city or cities; generally regarded as the suburbs.

own children Own children are sons and daughters, including stepchildren and adopted children, of the householder. The totals include never-married children living away from home in college dormitories.

owner occupied A housing unit is "owner occupied" if the owner lives in the unit, even if it is mortgaged or not fully paid for. A cooperative or condominium unit is "owner occupied" only if the owner lives in it. All other occupied units are classified as "renter occupied."

part-time employment Part-time is less than 35 hours of work per week in a majority of the weeks worked during the year.

percent change The change (either positive or negative) in a measure that is expressed as a proportion of the starting measure. When median income changes from $20,000 to $25,000, for example, this is a 25 percent increase.

percentage point change The change (either positive or negative) in a value which is already expressed as a percentage. When a labor force participation rate changes from 70 percent of 75 percent, for example, this is a 5 percentage point increase.

poverty level The official income threshold below which families and people are classified as living in poverty. The threshold rises each year with inflation and varies depending on family size and age of householder.

principal cities The largest cities in a metropolitan area are called the principal cities. The balance of a metropolitan area outside the principal cities is regarded as the "suburbs."

proportion or share The value of a part expressed as a percentage of the whole. If there are 4 million people aged 25 and 3 million of them are white, then the white proportion is 75 percent.

race Race is self-reported and can be defined in three ways. The "race alone" population comprises people who identify themselves as only one race. The "race in combination" population comprises people who identify themselves as more than one race, such as white and black. The "race, alone or in combination" population includes both those who identify themselves as one race and those who identify themselves as more than one race.

regions The four major regions and nine census divisions of the United States are the state groupings as shown below:

Northeast:
—New England: Connecticut, Maine, Massachusetts, New Hampshire, Rhode Island, and Vermont
—Middle Atlantic: New Jersey, New York, and Pennsylvania

Midwest:
—East North Central: Illinois, Indiana, Michigan, Ohio, and Wisconsin
—West North Central: Iowa, Kansas, Minnesota, Missouri, Nebraska, North Dakota, and South Dakota

South:
—South Atlantic: Delaware, District of Columbia, Florida, Georgia, Maryland, North Carolina, South Carolina, Virginia, and West Virginia
—East South Central: Alabama, Kentucky, Mississippi, and Tennessee
—West South Central: Arkansas, Louisiana, Oklahoma, and Texas

West:
—Mountain: Arizona, Colorado, Idaho, Montana, Nevada, New Mexico, Utah, and Wyoming
—Pacific: Alaska, California, Hawaii, Oregon, and Washington

renter occupied *See* Owner occupied.

Retirement Confidence Survey The RCS, sponsored by the Employee Benefit Research Institute (EBRI), the American Savings Education Council (ASEC), and Mathew Greenwald & Associates (Greenwald), is an annual survey of a nationally representative sample of 1,000 people aged 25 or older. Respondents are asked a core set of questions that have been asked since 1996, measuring attitudes and behavior towards retirement. Additional questions are also asked about current retirement issues.

rounding Percentages are rounded to the nearest tenth of a percent; therefore, the percentages in a distribution do not always add exactly to 100.0 percent. The totals, however, are always shown as 100.0. Moreover, individual figures are rounded to the nearest thousand without being adjusted to group totals, which are independently rounded; percentages are based on the unrounded numbers.

self-employment A person is categorized as self-employed if he or she was self-employed in the job held longest during the reference period. Persons who report self-employment from a second job are excluded, but those who report wage-and-salary income from a second job are included. Unpaid workers in family businesses are excluded. Self-employment statistics include only nonagricultural workers and exclude people who work for themselves in incorporated business.

sex ratio The number of men per 100 women.

suburbs *See* Outside principal city.

Survey of Consumer Finances The Survey of Consumer Finances is a triennial survey taken by the Federal Reserve Board. It collects data on the assets, debts, and net worth of American households. For the 2004 survey, the Federal Reserve Board interviewed a representative sample of 4,522 households.

unemployed Unemployed people are those who, during the survey period, had no employment but were available and looking for work. Those who were laid off from their jobs and were waiting to be recalled are also classified as unemployed.

white The "white" racial category includes many Hispanics (who may be of any race) unless the term "non-Hispanic white" is used.

Bibliography

Bianchi, Suzanne M., Robinson, John P., and Milkie, Melissa A., *Changing Rhythms of American Family Life* (New York: Russell Sage Foundation, 2006)

Bureau of the Census
Internet site http://www.census.gov
—2006 American Community Survey, Internet site http://factfinder.census.gov/home/saff/main.html?_lang=en
—2007 Current Population Survey Annual Social and Economic Supplement, Internet site http://pubdb3.census.gov/macro/032007/faminc/toc.htm
—A Child's Day: 2004 (Selected Indicators of Child Well-Being), Detailed Tables, Internet site http://www.census.gov/population/www/socdemo/2004_detailedtables.html
—America's Families and Living Arrangements, 2006, Internet site http://www.census.gov/population/www/socdemo/hh-fam/cps2006.html
—Current Population Surveys, Annual Social and Economic Supplement, Historical Income Tables, Internet site http://www.census.gov/hhes/www/income/histinc/incfamdet.html
—Families and Living Arrangements, Historical Tables—Households, Internet site http://www.census.gov/population/www/socdemo/hh-fam.html
—Population Estimates, Internet site http://www.census.gov/popest/national/asrh/

Bureau of Labor Statistics
Internet site http://www.bls.gov
—2006 Consumer Expenditure Survey, Internet site http://www.bls.gov/cex/home.htm
—Employment Characteristics of Families, Internet site http://www.bls.gov/news.release/famee.toc.htm

National Center for Education Statistics
Internet site http://nces.ed.gov
—*America's Children: Key National Indicators of Children's Well-Being, 2007*, Internet site http://childstats.gov/americaschildren/tables.asp
—*Digest of Education Statistics: 2007*, Internet site http://nces.ed.gov/programs/digest/d07/tables_2.asp#Ch2Sub1
—Early Childhood Longitudinal Study, Birth Cohort (ECLS-B), Internet site http://nces.ed.gov/pubsearch/pubsinfo.asp?pubid=2006002

National Center for Health Statistics
Internet site http://www.cdc.gov/nchs
—*Fertility, Contraception, and Fatherhood: Data on Men and Women from Cycle 6 of the 2002 National Survey of Family Growth,* Vital and Health Statistics, Series 23, No. 26, 2006; Internet site http://www.cdc.gov/nchs/nsfg.htm

Pew Research Center
Internet site http://pewresearch.org/
—*Families Drawn Together by Communications Revolution,* February 21, 2006, Internet site
http://pewsocialtrends.org/pubs/305/families-drawn-together-by-communication-revolution

Phi Delta Kappa/Gallup Poll
Internet site www.pdkintl.org
—*The 39th Annual Phi Delta Kappa/Gallup Poll of the Public's Attitudes Toward the Public Schools,* September 2007, Internet site www.pdkintl.org/kappan/k_v89/k0709pol.htm

Survey Documentation and Analysis, University of California, Berkeley
Internet site http://sda.berkeley.edu
—Computer-assisted Survey Methods Program, University of California, Berkeley, General Social Surveys, 1972-2006 Cumulative Data Files, Internet site http://sda.berkeley.edu/cgi-bin32/hsda?harcsda+gss06

Index

after-school care, 30
age
    attitude toward rewards of parenthood
        by, 82
    by ability to speak English, 56, 66
    of children in households, 8–9, 12–15
    of householders, 10, 12, 14, 20–21
    population by, 57–59, 83–99
American Indian public school students by
        state, 73–74
Asian
    age of children in households, 13, 15
    by state, 69–74, 83–99
    children in day care, 29
    college aspirations for children, 81
    family income, 33, 37
    households with children, 3, 5
    living arrangements of children, 49, 51
    number of children in households, 7, 11
    population, 54, 58–59, 69–72, 83–99
    public school students, 73–74
attitudes
    of fathers, 77, 79–80
    toward childrearing, 18
    toward children's standard of living, 19
    toward rewards of parenthood, 78, 82
    toward public schools, 9
    toward working women, 17

Baby Boom, 16–21, 22
bilingual, 56, 66
black
    age of children in households, 13, 15
    attitude toward childrearing, 19
    attitude toward rewards of parenthood, 82
    by state, 69–74, 83–99
    children in day care, 29
    college aspirations for children, 81
    family income, 33, 37
    households with children, 3, 5
    living arrangements of children, 49–51
    number of children in households, 7, 11
    population, 54, 58–59, 69–72, 83–99
    public school students, 73–74
    spending, 55, 60–62

childrearing, attitude toward, 18
college, parental aspirations for, 78

day care, 24, 29–30

educational attainment
    attitude toward rewards of parenthood
        by, 82
    college aspirations by, 81
    day care use by, 29
employment status
    day care use by, 29
    of mothers, 24, 28
    of parents, 23, 27
English, ability to speak, 56, 66

fathers. *See* Men.
female-headed families
    by age, 20–21
    by generation, 22
    children living in, 48–51
    employment status, 23, 27
    historical trend, 4
    income of, 32, 35–36

Generation X, 16–21, 22
grandchildren
    living with grandparents, 52
    percent of people with, 9

Hispanic
    age of children in households, 13, 15
    attitude toward childrearing, 19
    attitude toward rewards of parenthood, 82
    by state, 69–74, 83–99
    children in day care, 29
    college aspirations for children, 81
    family income, 33, 37
    households with children, 3, 5
    living arrangements of children, 49–51
    number of children in households, 7, 9, 11
    population, 54, 58–59, 69–72, 83–99
    public school students, 73–74
    spending, 55, 63–65
homeownership, college aspirations by
        status, 81